You're Killing Me Here!

WHEN WIN-WIN NEGOTIATION DOESN'T WORK

by

Steve Reilly

ISBN: 9780615307701 (paperback)

A Pulp Non-Fiction Publication

For Rocky and Maddy, *best friends forever*

Table of Contents

Enough With The Win-Win Already

The fifth-most-successful business book of all time and number-one negotiation book by a large, large margin is *Getting to Yes, Negotiating Agreement Without Giving In* by William Ury and Roger Fisher, published in 1981. The book initiated an extraordinary shift in corporate America's negotiation philosophy from zero-sum to win-win. What was once considered an adversarial, often-contentious struggle between buyers and sellers shifted to a collaborative, problem-solving mindset as it became clear that the zero-sum negotiating philosophy of "I win only if you lose" did not always fit in a world of business interdependencies and cooperation. The authors recognized that, although zero-sum negotiators may achieve short-term financial goals, their heavy-handed tactics often damage longer-term, more valuable relationships.

For more than 15 years, I was a Master Certified Instructor for the Negotiating to Yes Seminar (*NTY*) based on William Ury and Roger Fisher's best-selling book. During that period, I facilitated *NTY* workshops in almost every industry, country, and business situation to audiences of manufacturing line supervisors, sales teams, contract administrators, executives, and buyers. I also presented the *Getting to Yes* concepts at executive conferences, sales meetings, and corporate retreats.

The corporate version of the workshop consists of two days of classroom lectures, videos, role-plays, negotiation situations, and a proprietary negotiation planner. At the time, corporate training departments and sales managers selected the *NTY* program to improve their people's (mostly salespeople) negotiation skills. The average cost of the workshop was $15,000 per session and non-negotiable. (It always strikes me as ironic that the company with the most popular negotiating program had a non-negotiable pricing policy.)

SMART QUESTIONS, STUPID ANSWERS

Over time, I became more and more curious about whether the substantial amounts of money companies shelled out for the NTY program translated into better deals and better skills. The fact that, through the years, seminar participants raised the same questions, again and again, fueled my suspicions.

After comparing notes with other workshop leaders, it became apparent that the same questions came up in every NTY seminar, regardless of the audience, industry, or situation. We all encountered the same resistance to the ideas and techniques of the workshop.

Questions like "What number do you start with?" or "When and how much do you concede on the first counteroffer?" or "How do you respond to a request for your best and final offer?" were never satisfactorily addressed in the *NTY* workshop or book. In response to this pushback, the seminar designers equipped us with a set of "canned" answers as ammunition to fend off the workshop participants who just didn't get it.

The most common question was, "What if the customer

doesn't want to play win-win?" to which our cavalier response was, "Then maybe you should find a customer who will."

When asked, "What number do I start with?" our canned answer was, "Win-win isn't about offers and counteroffers. It's about relationships."

I became suspicious that our proprietary scripted answers left workshop participants with less than useful tools. In response to my suspicions, I dug deeper into the world of negotiation. I spent a substantial amount of time and energy, absorbing the plethora of other negotiation books and theories. I hoped to find some expert who would enlighten me on addressing Ury and Fisher's approach's inadequacies.

There weren't any. Most books written by negotiation experts failed to answer these same questions. Making my living in sales since graduate school, I knew from first-hand experience that salespeople deal with questions like these every day. Their world is filled with customers who refuse to play anything except hardball; selling can be an unforgiving business with unforgiving customers.

My participants' questions were left unaddressed by the most famous and popular negotiation gurus. While some books answered one or two questions, many answered none at all. My list of questions grew as their list of answers shrank.

WAKE-UP CALL

Then a client, the largest private health insurer in America, asked my help negotiating contracts with medical services providers. Every year, hospitals and insurers come together to hammer out contracts that determine the reimbursement rates for medical services provided to their health plan members.

These negotiations almost always begin with seemingly impossible gaps between the hospital and insurer positions and a looming contract deadline. If these contracts expire, thousands of people lose their medical care, and an insurance company is left with a potentially fatal hole in its revenue for years to come.

This was negotiating with real consequences.

Almost nothing from my *Getting to Yes* experience prepared me for the no-holds-barred, knockdown, drag-out process of hospital contracting where no one left unscathed, and everyone bled at least a bit. When I tried to apply the win/win methodology, I soon realized that a win-win approach made little difference. The *Getting to Yes* techniques had almost no application to the reality of these contentious, high-stakes, and business-critical negotiations.

While fine theoretically, the collaborative strategy fell apart when encountering a side that played hardball. Some paid lip service to win-win principles, but, in the end, it came down to defending your position and giving ground very, very grudgingly.

The other side didn't come prepared to share their interests or cooperate in these types of negotiations. Their goal is to get as much as possible at the expense of the other side and the most important skill is the ability to take a punch, get up, and punch back.

Surprisingly, and despite what sometimes seemed like impossible odds, 99 out of every 100 negotiations ended up with a mutually disagreeable contract of one year in length. This was considered a success despite both parties leaving bloodied and exhausted. And it guaranteed that the same down and dirty process would start over as soon as nine months after the contract went into effect.

In a sort of karmic payback, the same questions posed by

my seminar participants were now being asked of me by every hospital administrator and financial officer I encountered. My canned responses were useless.

But now, unlike in a seminar classroom, my answers had real consequences.

Hospital contract negotiations have hundreds, even thousands, of items "in play," and conceding in one area means having to make up for it in another. They are some of the most complicated negotiation situations anyone will ever encounter. Health insurers have entire departments whose only job is to run contract modeling software to determine whether a hospital agreement will cover the health plan's anticipated costs. I learned a lot.

Lessons Learned

Although it was intellectually challenging and emotionally exhausting, I emerged a better negotiator and workshop instructor. I didn't so much *learn* these lessons as much as I was *taught* them by hard knocks and working through the most challenging negotiation situations I had ever encountered.

I learned more about negotiation in six months than in all my years teaching Ury and Fisher's approach.

There were many important lessons, but three stand out to achieve better outcomes in hardball negotiation situations.

Lesson One
If you use win-win techniques with
hardball negotiators, you will lose.

Despite the global success of Getting to Yes, many complain (myself included) that although a win-win strategy is noble in purpose, it is increasingly difficult to execute as the stakes rise. A collaborative approach does not work in difficult negotiation situations and, at times, limits your chances of reaching a satisfying agreement. Ury and Fisher's method works well when both sides share multiple interests, especially when they trust each other. When a collaborative negotiator encounters another with the same philosophy, the outcome is often a win for both.

But being skilled at win-win negotiation does not prepare you for the challenges of hard bargaining. Being "fluent" solely in win-win limits your success to others who share your philosophy; it puts you in a weaker position with those who don't.

Unlike the hopeful philosophy espoused in Getting to Yes, hardball negotiators don't think about interests or relationships; they see salespeople as replaceable, products as commodities, and negotiations as transactions. They will play win-win, but only when they have nothing to lose.

Every day in every industry in every part of the world, customers ask salespeople to make crucial pricing decisions on the spot. Salespeople don't have the luxury of time to think about the short- and long-term impact of their decisions or fill out a three-page negotiation planner.

Customers want the best price, and they want it now.

To respond to those challenges effectively, salespeople need a pragmatic strategy that helps them hold their ground and achieve better outcomes. Getting to Yes may be useful when negotiating with a landlord (an example used by Ury in the book) or reaching an agreement on a strategic arms treaty (another Ury example) but makes few connections to the day-to-day business world.

Don't get me wrong.

I highly recommend it. It is an excellent book on the benefits of reaching collaborative agreements, if only for the idea that parties who reach agreements tend to be more committed to terms and conditions. But it provides little guidance when trying to hold your ground against an adversarial opponent. And though supporters of the win-win approach believe it is possible to break-down and break-through the other side's antagonistic wall, I consider that a bit naïve, especially in sales.

Negotiation approaches fall on a continuum from zero-sum (hardball) to win-win (cooperation). At one end of the continuum are tough customers with uncompromising, dog-eat-dog negotiation philosophies. Zero-sum negotiations are unavoidable in the sales world and are characterized by customers who see negotiation as something to "win" at the other side's expense. They assume that the size of the pie is fixed, with the strongest side ending up with the biggest slice. The skills of compromise and cooperation are mostly useless as tough buyers don't show their cards unless they have to and believe they have the upper hand even when they don't.

On the other end of the spectrum are the win-win negotiators whose primary objective is preserving the relationship and sharing the pot. Both sides typically trust each other and are open to brainstorming and creativity to expand the pie and find a solution that satisfies both sides' interests. Maintaining the relationship takes precedence.

Now, we could have a substantial discussion about which is better, but unfortunately, neither of us gets to choose.

The customer makes that choice.

And as I said, a negotiator "fluent" in only win-win is at a distinct disadvantage. Of course, a negotiator who is only fluent in "hardball" is also at a disadvantage, but their disadvantage is different. It is much more difficult for a win-win salesperson to recover ground lost to a tough customer than for a hardball negotiator to move to a more cooperative approach. If you can play both win/win and hardball, you can adapt your approach to each situation's needs.

Most negotiations are not one or the other, completely. Negotiators move along this spectrum as trust is built and lost during back-and-forth bargaining. But in my experience, the best negotiators play hardball first, win-win second. I begin my negotiations assuming the other side wants to play win-win while keeping my cards close to the vest and protecting my interests. Eventually, I get a feel for how open the other side is to "playing nice." I then move from a cautious, zero-sum approach toward a more collaborative discussion as my opponents' intentions become clearer.

For instance, hospital contractors often open negotiations by telling insurance companies their hospital is losing money. They use this tactic to convince the insurer that the hospital needs to maximize its reimbursement for financial reasons. Basically, it is positioning. What hospitals don't know is that I can read their annual reports better than most people and quickly determine if the hospital is truly in financial straits or hiding profits with capital investments to maintain their "nonprofit" status.

Knowing that hospital administrators embellish, I advise my clients to be cautious until they build trust in other ways. This may or may not happen but starting with a cautious but optimistic approach helps protect the insurer's interests. Being skeptical of the other sides' positioning statements is the right approach, at least at the beginning. Skepticism serves you well with a hard-bargaining opponent; hope is not a strategy.

The win-win ideology promoted and taught by "experts" leaves many salespeople vulnerable to hardball tactics and strategies. In collaborative negotiations, sharing your interests is considered fair and even encouraged. But in zero-sum negotiations, showing your cards is foolish and naive.

Take the situation of purchasing a car. The salesperson may seem friendly, open, and helpful, but the dealership is interested in getting as much money for their inventory as possible, regardless of the collateral damage to the relationship. That's just the way it works. It isn't wise to share your interests with a car dealer, at least at first. Your new car buying experience is statistically related to the brand of automobile you choose but not which dealership you use; there is not much incentive for dealers to "play nice."

And despite what experts say, it is not always possible to reach mutually agreeable outcomes. More times than not, one side gets screwed. So, whereas the first lesson is that playing win-win all the time can hurt you, the second lesson is a bit more complicated.

Lesson Two
The most important difference between one negotiation and another is not the item being negotiated.

Negotiation experts will tell you that all negotiations are the same, "If you've seen one, you've seen them all," and that their proprietary approach will work for every situation regardless of the industry. To prove their point, they use examples from strategic arms talks, labor negotiations, or other non-business situations to show similarities from one to another. This helps them argue that their techniques are transferrable from industry to industry and from situation to situation. In the end, it allows them to sell more books and workshops.

This disconnect between the industry and negotiation strategy is why, despite their claims, many seminars fail to significantly improve negotiation skills.

Every negotiation is different, and skills that work in one do not necessarily work in others. It is a mistake for experts to equate all negotiations. But they are mistaken for the reason that would most likely never occur to them.

The factor that most differentiates one negotiation from another is not the product or service being haggled over. It isn't the negotiation teams or team members on either side. It isn't the amount of money on the table, either. Each of these factors contributes to a negotiation outcome, but they are not the essential difference.

The most important factor that differentiates one negotiation from another is complexity.

Complexity is defined by the number of interdependent variables "in play." The number of items in play in a negotiation determines which skills and techniques are required. For simple negotiations with a single item in play like price, tips and techniques may get you a better deal. Simple, short, transactional negotiations like buying something off Craigslist or eBay don't require much negotiation expertise. Making one counteroffer and having it accepted or rejected can be the entire negotiation.

But in more complex negotiations, the most critical skill is strategy. Complex negotiations demand a more strategic approach and, therefore, different skills.

LAUNDRY LISTS

The alternative to Ury and Fisher's approach was pioneered by Dr. Chester Karass (think airline magazines) in his book Effective Negotiation. His seminar, based on the book, is one of the most popular business training programs available. (Another expert whose prices are non-negotiable). His book and seminar teach salespeople various tips and techniques useful for bargaining with customers. Basically, his is a series of unconnected techniques for countering negotiating tricks with quirky names like good-guy/bad-guy and the "nibbler." This "laundry list" of tactics is useful when negotiating simple, transactional, single-issue items; car, cell phone bill discount, flea market items, etc.

But in large negotiations, these "tips" can make a negotiator look amateurish and interfere with a well-thought-out strategy. In a complex negotiation with multiple factors, multiple decision-makers, and interdependencies between terms and conditions, a more sophisticated strategy is needed.

When you buy a car, there are relatively few items to be worked out in the negotiation process; most car deals can be completed in a couple of hours. Purchasing a $20 million Caterpillar mining truck is much more complicated and takes longer. The list of items "in play" can include price, delivery, service, after-market parts inventory, hourly shop repair fees, financing interest rates, payment plans, in-field emergency service, and replacement equipment. This level of negotiating takes thought and planning.

A three-year hospital contract includes inpatient and outpatient billing, Medicare reimbursement, Medicaid reimbursement, private insurer, and out-of-network reimbursement rates. Almost all hospital contracts contain "carve-outs" for high-expense procedures like trauma, neonatal care, and sepsis. And these carve-outs, often reimbursed with a completely different methodology than routine procedures, are negotiated separately and then figured into the overall reimbursement totals.

All large insurers like Aetna, Blue Cross/Blue Shield, and United HealthCare have large contract pricing departments whose sole purpose is to run pricing modeling software to determine how conceding in one particular section of the contract will impact overall profitability. This is a negotiation at its most business-critical and complex application. (Some of you may be thinking that this is the problem with our healthcare system. And you would be right.)

Strategy vs. Tactics

The other shortcoming of popular negotiation approaches is that they don't scale. Because negotiations vary widely in complexity, techniques need to be scalable. To become a good negotiator, you need a negotiation strategy that works for the simplest and most complex situations.

Because most negotiating gurus' examples and techniques are applied to single-issue negotiations, it is difficult, if not impossible, to integrate those same techniques into large, complex negotiations, especially when large sums of money are at risk. Therefore, negotiation success depends on applying the correct strategy to the particular negotiation phase. Strategy trumps tactics every time.

Tactics are the things you do while at the bargaining table.

Tactics are the techniques you use when engaged in the actual back-and-forth of negotiation. You use tactics to implement your strategy – things like offers and counteroffers, bluffs, brinksmanship, and so on. Presenting a counteroffer, challenging their opening bid, and other tactics help you implement your strategy and achieve your negotiation goals.

Strategy is related to tactics but different.

Strategy are the things you do away from the negotiation table.

It is the overarching objective or goal of your negotiation, like maintaining the company's Average Selling Price (ASP), penetrating the market, or establishing or reinforcing your company and product's brand. Strategy consists of pre-negotiation analysis and planning, evaluation and re-evaluation of counteroffers, and changes to your tactics triggered by the other side's actions.

Strategy impacts tactics, and tactics impacts strategy. Using a football analogy, if a coach wants to establish the running game (strategy), his tactics will include a good offensive line with the ability to open up running lanes and tight ends to block on the outside (tactics) using plays that maximize the team's ground assets. But if the team falls behind by three touchdowns early in the game, the coach must revisit his strategy and revise the tactical plan.

Unfortunately, many negotiators fall behind but continue to run the ball.

I use the concept of strategy by asking sales teams to "sidebar" before answering customer questions or responding to their demands. A sidebar is a simple and effective technique of taking a "time out" for a quick huddle to make sure everyone is on the same page. It slows down the thought process and determines the best way to react while better serving their company's interests. (How do you know your team needs to take a sidebar? When someone kicks you under the table.)

Negotiation strategies that rely on complex models are mostly useless for simple, transactional negotiation situations. Taking two or three days in a classroom, filling out negotiation strategy planners, and working through binders while negotiating agreements for products not related to your industry, is not a well-spent use of your time or your company's money.

Just have your people read a good negotiation book.

But sales organizations with big-ticket, complex products with many terms and conditions need to understand strategy and tactics, and their interplay. This interdependence of strategy and tactics impacts the skills a salesperson needs to become an expert negotiator. A more strategic and deliberate approach is critical to reaching acceptable deals. The interdependence of strategy and tactics is one of the most important concepts in this book.

Lesson Three
It is not that difficult to become a better negotiator.

With a couple of fundamental principles, strategies, and phrases, anyone can reach better deals even when up against hardball opponents. Becoming a better negotiator is relatively easy, and if you begin using the phrase "You're killing me here!" you already are.

This book combines my experience as a salesperson and sales manager with the insights I've gained from 15 years of consulting and training with global corporations in the areas of sales, negotiation, and leadership.

My approach is not based on theories about human nature, nuclear arms strategies, or labor union bargaining tactics. Neither is it a "laundry list" of tips and techniques. It is a step-by-step process following the flow of most negotiations from the first offer to contract signing. I wrote this book at my clients' requests for help dealing with hardball negotiators. My primary purpose is to provide you with a simple, proven process for holding your ground against purchasing agents, procurement officers, buyers, customers, and bosses with whom win-win doesn't work.

My process works when win-win doesn't.

This Is Not Negotiating

In my years as an instructor, when asked to define negotiation, I regurgitated Ury's scripted answer, "Negotiation is back and forth communication when some interests are shared, and some interests are opposed." Experts sometimes make things more complicated than they need to be.

The definition of negotiation is clear and straightforward. Negotiation is the middle ground between capitulation and stonewalling; it is the space between giving in or refusing to negotiate.

A negotiating party must be willing to give and take. If the price is "set," there is no "give and take," there is only "take it or leave it." One side may think they are negotiating, but if the other side doesn't play, they aren't playing, either. On the other hand, when salespeople give in without any back-and-forth or capitulate, they aren't negotiating either though they may think they are.

People want something concrete to deal with in a negotiation, and by definition, the price is not concrete until it is negotiated. It can be the ultimate exercise in frustration tolerance, and some would rather have a quick agreement even if money is left on the table. A high-stakes negotiation demands patience and the ability to deal with ambiguity.

This Is Negotiating

Several years ago, I had the opportunity to attend an auto convention with a client that builds and manages dealer websites, driving traffic, and business over the web. At one point, I found myself in a meeting room with several dealer finance people. I took the opportunity to ask them about car dealer negotiations.

"Which customer gets the best deal?"

"What do you mean?"

"What type of customer walks out of the dealership with the lowest price? Is it the person who researches all possible options on the internet and comes in with all the data to back him up? Or is it the person who comes in with a make, model, and price and asks you to match it, or they'll go somewhere else?"

Their unanimous response surprised me.

"The customer who gets the best deal is the one who comes into the dealership unhappy with the price and leaves the dealership unhappy with the price. No matter how much of a deal you give them, they are never satisfied."

"Do you know whether that's a deliberate strategy or just a person who is by nature never satisfied?" I asked.

"We never know. They don't tell us. That would be showing their hand."

"So, they work you as much as you work them."

"Absolutely. But the difference is that they stay in the game. They don't walk away or make unreasonable demands."

So, according to some of the most experienced dealmakers, the best negotiators aren't those who have a bunch of tricks up their sleeves, regardless of what the experts tell you. The best people at making deals, at least in the car business, are those who stay in the game until they get what they want or at least something they can live with.

People don't like negotiating because it can mean that they have to deal with an adversarial opponent and put up with haggling. Some deal with their discomfort by avoiding the back-and-forth entirely. My father paid full sticker price for a Ford Pinto station wagon and to this day believes he got a good deal. His definition of a good deal is not having to negotiate.

Still, others cave to customer demands without fighting. Many salespeople capitulate to customer demands to avoid the back-and-forth and lose sales or profit.

When you give in or walk away, you are not negotiating.

Not Everything Is Negotiable

Some years ago, I had the opportunity to work with Ekins, a Nike Corporation sales team. (Ekins is Nike spelled backward.) The Ekins salespeople's job is to sell the Nike product line to smaller retailers, family-owned chains of three stores or less. One of their most difficult challenges is communicating the Nike Market Segmentation Strategy (MSS) to their customers. Nike uses its MSS to protect and enhance the brand by allocating certain athletic shoe lines to specific market segments based on strength and visibility.

At that time, the Air Jordan shoe line was at the peak of its popularity. You might recall that Nike introduced a new version of the Jordan shoe every quarter. And for kids to stay "cool" with their peers, they had to have the new model on the day it was released. (At one point, Nike changed the Air Jordan new model release date from the first day of each quarter to the first Saturday of each quarter. This was to deal with the complaint from school systems that saw a spike in truancy when NIKE released the new model on a school day.)

Because of NIKE's strategy, the Air Jordan line was only available to Elite Nike retailers, including major sporting good chains like Footlocker, Athletic Attic, Champs, and Nike-owned stores. Retailers could count on a jump in sales every quarter from the Air Jordan release – some retailers, that is.

For obvious reasons, this did not please the small sports equipment chains. The owners tried every trick in the negotiating book to secure an inventory of Air Jordan's, but the simple fact remained that this was "non-negotiable." It was a waste of time and energy because it was not going to happen.

Some things are non-negotiable. If, the other side doesn't play, you aren't playing, either. And besides, trying to negotiate everything seems slightly pathological or, at the very least, highly irritating to friends and family.

COMMON MISTAKES

Trying to take on hardball negotiators without understanding the two most ubiquitous negotiation blunders might be an exercise in futility. These two damaging mistakes are commonly made by both the greenest and the most experienced salespeople.

THE *MOST* COMMON NEGOTIATING MISTAKE
Giving Ground Too Easily

Hundreds of sales managers share the same complaint about their people's negotiating skills; they give in too early and too easily; that their salespeople leave more money on the table than necessary. Bad enough in a win-win negotiation; it is disastrous with hardball negotiators. Giving in to a zero-sum negotiator incentivizes them to ask for more.

Perhaps this is because most salespeople have incentive-based compensation and a quota to achieve. It is natural to want to avoid anything that might lead to the loss of a sale. But throwing a heavily discounted price on the table in hopes of making a sale is backward selling. It is the wrong way to begin any negotiation and weakens your ability to hold your ground.

This happens when salespeople start negotiating before they are done selling.

THE *SECOND MOST* COMMON NEGOTIATING MISTAKE
Conceding and Getting Nothing in Return

Perhaps because of the overwhelming influence of the win-win philosophy, salespeople give away price, term, conditions, and more in hopes of getting the other side to play nice and return the favors. Making concessions without a counter-concession in a zero-sum negotiation can be devastating to your desired outcome. It's like feeding meat to a carnivore, hoping it will eventually become a vegetarian.

It isn't going to happen.

Some negotiation philosophies preach that making any concession is a mistake. I'm afraid I have to disagree. Trading a concession to get something of value can be a powerful negotiating strategy with more upside benefits than downside risks.

Karrass spends more time than necessary focusing on techniques for responding to eleventh-hour requests for additional concessions called "nibbles." His defense essentially boils down to starting the negotiation over or walking away from the deal. Neither of these reactions is necessary if you understand the reason customers make these demands. Customers make so-called "nibbles" because salespeople don't teach them that concessions come with a cost; that to get a concession, they need to make a concession.

Demanding concession reciprocity quickly stops this petty ploy.

CRUCIAL SKILLS

The two most common negotiation mistakes can be countered by learning the two most important negotiation skills.

THE *MOST* IMPORTANT NEGOTIATING SKILL
Holding Your Ground

If the most common negotiation *mistake* is giving ground too easily then the most important negotiating *skill* is the ability to hold your ground. You've heard the saying, "Once a price is on the table, the next person who speaks loses." While silence can be an effective tactic in some situations, there is a better way.

Once your price is on the table, your next step is to defend it. The better you defend your number, the better you hold your ground. Important in any negotiation, it becomes critical when up against tough bargainers.

Price is related to value and salespeople who sell on value are good at holding their ground. They know that the greater emphasis they put on value pays off in more negotiating power.

A strong value proposition can determine how close you end up to your asking price.

The best defense is a good offense.

The *Second Most* Important Negotiation Skill
Trading Concessions

If the second most common *mistake* is making concessions, the second most important *skill* is trading concessions. Contrary to popular negotiation theory, conceding is not necessarily a bad tactic as long as you insist on reciprocal concessions. Reciprocity ensures a more mutually acceptable agreement with better compliance and accountability. When both sides give, there is a greater commitment to the outcome.

A negotiation strategy that integrates reciprocal concessions quickly improves profitability and commitment to contract terms.

This Book's Objective

Because the interplay between strategy and tactics is so critical, each chapter begins with a higher-level, more complex discussion of strategy, then provide tactics specific to the negotiation phase. In other words, I have connected tactics to the specific strategy of each Phase; First Offer Strategy-Tactics, Trading Concessions Strategy-Tactics, Best and Final Offer Strategy-Tactics. This establishes a foundation which can be applied to many different negotiating situations.

This book is intended for sales organizations. My primary audience is salespeople who encounter difficult customers, procurement officers, and other "buyers" of products and services.

The negotiation situations I use are mostly based in the selling world. While some skills may apply to non-sales situations, my intention is not to dilute the ideas by attempting to broaden my audience.

The Rocky Story

A Math Problem

At the end of fourth grade, my youngest, Maddy, was having problems with math. She struggled with her homework, with her tests, with her math flashcards. She is a great student and hard worker but has a few problems with focus and understanding.

As the summer began, she was looking forward to time off from her studies; I thought the three months of summer might be a good time to work on her math skills. We went to the local bookstore and found a math-skills workbook. Maddy groaned when she saw the 100 pages of math puzzles, riddles, and word problems.

We sat down, and I explained that math skills are a crucial foundation for other subjects; that math opens up many different learning avenues, like biology, physics, and physiology. Of course, I explained this in fourth-grader terms. She bought my argument but still wanted to spend the summer focused on play, not school.

So, we made a deal.

I told her that if she completed two math pages each day, she could have anything she wanted, providing her math scores went up at the beginning of the school year.

"Anything I want, Dad?"

I stopped for a minute and then plunged in headfirst.

"Yes, honey. Anything you want and can legally have. So, you know, like a car is out. But anything reasonable is fine."

She worked very hard; two pages a day, sometimes three. She added up our restaurant checks, helped balance my checkbook, and counting change became a regular ritual. She finished the workbook in early August with the rest of the summer to relax.

I was cautiously optimistic about her progress at the beginning of the Fall semester but had to wait until the first parent/teacher conference to find out whether her hard work had paid off in better math skills. Her school mixed classes so Maddy had the same teacher from fourth grade. She shared with me that Maddy had come a long way and her math scores were among the best in the class. It was a big relief as it would be for any parent.

But it meant I had a promise to keep.

Maddy met me at the door when I arrived home from the conference.

"Did she tell you how I was doing, Dad?"

"She did, honey. She said you are one of the best math students in the class."

"I told you I could do it."

"I know, honey. You worked hard, and I am very proud of you."

"Remember your promise, Dad? That I could have anything I want."

"Within reason, honey," I added.

"I know, but you PROMISED!"

"I know, honey, and Dad keeps his promises." At least I try to.

"I know what I want."

Apprehensively, I asked, "What is it, honey?"

"I want a puppy. I want a puppy I can have with me all the time. He can stay with me when I am at your house and stay with me when I go to Moms. Is that all right?"

"So, you want a dog then."

"No, Dad, I want a puppy."

"Okay, a puppy. Are you sure you want one enough to take care of it?"

"Yes, Dad. I promise to walk it and feed it and clean up its . . . you know . . . stuff." Cute.

"I made the promise, honey, and I will keep it. Tomorrow we start looking for a dog."

"You mean a puppy."

"Yes, I mean a puppy."

And our quest for a dog, I mean puppy, began.

Chapter 1

First Offers Strategy and Tactics

The hospital administrator pushed a note typed on official hospital letterhead across the table.

"What is this?" I asked.

"It's our termination letter. If we don't get what we want, we'll let the contract expire, and you will be S.O.L. We don't have to do business with you. You need us more than we need you."

A termination letter is a formal document required by law for hospitals to communicate to a medical insurance company that the current agreement will be allowed to expire at the end of its contract period. When and if a hospital contract is allowed to "term," the members (patients) must be notified that they need to make arrangements with other doctors and/or hospitals to maintain coverage — a very disruptive decision for people and their health care providers. In short, it is a threat to the insurer to provide a better deal...or else.

Stupid move, I thought to myself.

The administrator was acting tough, hoping to put us on the defensive. It was obvious he hadn't completely thought through this not-very-veiled threat. He didn't realize that using his "term" letter as a bargaining chip would only work if the hospital was willing to follow through – and it wasn't.

There was too much at risk. Walking away would cost him and his hospital much more than it would cost my client. And if he had to pull that piece of paper back to his side of the table, his leverage would be gone. But he carried on despite the amateur ploy.

"What's your first offer?" he asked smugly.

"We don't know yet. We have some questions."

"We don't have time for questions. Just tell us what you want, and we'll make you an offer you can't refuse." He smiled god-fatherly.

"Sorry, we can't do that until we have an idea what your hospital is looking for. We need more information." I held my ground.

"Okay, we are looking for a 15-percent increase over last year,"

I stopped and thought for a minute.

"If you don't mind me asking, how did you come up with a 15-percent increase?" I asked as politely as I could.

"I do mind you asking. That's what we want, and that's that"

"Okay, I can understand that your hospital thinks it needs a 15-percent increase, but why that number? Why not 14 or 16 percent?"

He was getting irritated, which was fine with me.

"It's simple; our hospital is getting crushed by labor costs. Our nursing expenses increased 15 percent last year. We need to make up for that with your contract. You can do that much math, right?" he asked condescendingly.

"I see. But then how much do your nursing expenses make up of your total hospital budget?"

"What does that matter? What do you mean?" His eyes shifted to his colleagues, nervously.

"Well, if your nursing expenses are increasing by 15 percent but only make up 10 percent of your total costs, then you are asking us to cover a lot more than just nursing costs. A 15-percent increase across the board would be much more revenue than just the increase in your nursing costs. I don't see how that is fair."

"It doesn't matter if it is fair. We just want a 15-percent increase."

"Right. But I can't propose a 15 percent increase in payments unless I have a good reason."

That rattled him. Now he was on the defensive. Glancing nervously at his colleagues, he asked, "Uh, can you give us five minutes? We need to discuss a couple of things."

"Sure. We'll wait outside the conference room until you are ready. Take all the time you need."

His team looked a bit sheepish as we gave them their privacy.

Five minutes stretched to 20. Finally, they called us back into the conference room.

The administrator had his tail between his legs.

"Maybe we got off on the wrong foot. We want to come clean and start over again if you let us." His tone had changed significantly, almost contrite.

"No problem. I am sure we can work something out." Always a good idea to let a negotiator save face when they are eating crow.

"Here is our proposal. We need to increase your payments for our most expensive procedures. Our costs on trauma, NICU [neonatal intensive care unit), and sepsis cases are killing us. Can you help us out there?"

"I think we can, but if you don't mind, we'd also like to look at some areas to reduce our costs while making you whole in your more expensive patient areas," I said.

"Sounds great. Let's dig into the numbers."

From then on, the negotiation became more of a discussion than a disagreement. We were able to reach a deal, not a perfect deal, but a deal.

First Offers Strategy and Tactics

Most negotiation experts separate negotiating from selling; they treat them as independent subjects needing different skills. That could be because most have little in-the-field selling experience and were never in a position that required them to make a sales number (quota). They think nuclear arms talks, labor relations, and other non-sales negotiation situations easily relate to selling situations. There may be similarities, but sales is a different animal.

What these experts don't understand is that selling and negotiation are inseparable and critically dependent upon each other; that the outcome of one depends on how good you are at the other. This concept is foreign to those who never "carried a bag."

Here is the unbreakable link between selling and negotiating.

There are only two ways to narrow the gap between the lower price a buyer wants to pay and the higher price a seller wants to charge. Either you convince the buyer that the value of your product or service offsets the price difference (that's called selling), or you trade concessions until you reach a mutually agreeable or disagreeable deal (that's called negotiating). Understanding this link is both basic and crucial to becoming a better negotiator.

Salespeople who sell on price put a number on the table too early. Once that happens, it is difficult to recover the sales process; negotiations become about how much or how little the customer pays, instead of value. Many salespeople make the excuse that their customers demand a price before they will let the sales process begin. They argue that their job is to respond to customers' R.F.P.s (Requests for Proposal), RFQ (Request for Quotation), or make a bid on a competitive proposal leaving little room to negotiate.

I want to be clear.

Responding to an R.F.P. or bid is not negotiating. If there is no back-and-forth, there is no negotiation. Responding to a sales quote may require financial analysis, but no negotiation skill will help you get a better deal. Differentiation takes place during the sales process, not the negotiation process. This makes positioning value before the RFP critical to your success.

Skilled salespeople ignore pricing requests until they establish enough value to justify their price. Salespeople who reach more successful outcomes are good at selling and negotiating. Salespeople who are good at positioning their products' value put themselves and their companies in better negotiation positions. Those who do a poor job of differentiating almost always find themselves disadvantaged in holding their ground against customers. Salespeople who sell on price reach less profitable agreements, if they reach any at all. They make it more difficult for themselves.

First Offers Strategy

But after all the positioning and blustering is done, for any negotiation to begin, one side needs to put a number out there. Sometimes that person is you.

Determining the price you start with is the first and most important strategic negotiation decision. Another common question in win-win workshops is, "What number do you start with?" The most common "expert" answer is, "It depends," which leads to the next question, "What are the things it depends on?" which always leads to the frustrating answer, "Even that depends." Those answers may be good advice in a collaborative negotiation; they are useless in zero-sum. Negotiations are about price, and no matter what you say or do, customers insist on having something to work with; they want a number.

So, the question remained, and my search for a definitive answer was fruitless for a long time.

Then one day, in an especially contentious negotiation over the price of wire cable, I found the answer. My client, the salesperson's company, manufactures and supplies wire cable to telecom, construction, aerospace, and other industries. I was interested in seeing how negotiations play out in a highly commoditized market; when most customers know your competitors' pricing and customers have plenty of alternatives.

After all, cable is cable — or so I thought.

At one point in the meeting, the customer said in frustration, "Your price is just not competitive. We want to do business with you, but at this price, I'm not sure it's going to work." I looked at the salesperson to see how he would respond.

His unexpected response gave me the long-sought-after answer in one short and sweet counterpunch. "Our price is fair and reasonable, and let me tell you why…"

The best response to the question "What number do I start with?" isn't a specific number, making a counteroffer at a lower price, pushing it off as a decision for upper management, or even silently staring at the other side across the negotiation table. It isn't the evasive response, "It depends," either.

The number you start with is the number you can defend. Full stop.

It seems obvious now, but I never found this simple defense in any negotiation book or seminar.

Let me use a simple example to illustrate the power of this tool.

Suppose you have a car to sell. You determine its Kelley Blue Book (KBB) value is $15,000. Having taken excellent care of this particular automobile, you decide to list it for $2,000 more than KBB price, $17,000. Next, let's suppose you receive a call from an interested party who says, "I'm interested in your car, but the Kelley Blue Book is only $15,000. Can you reduce your price?"

A poor negotiator's response is, "Well, would you be willing to pay $16,500?" By conceding too early, you gave away a substantial amount of profit for no reason.

The best response is, "This car is worth $17,000, and let me tell you why…."

The stronger your value proposition, the better your argument, the better you are at holding your ground. Defending your price is essential to satisfying your interests and improving your negotiation outcomes. Having a strong ending to the phrase "Our price is fair and reasonable, and let me tell you why…" puts you on the offensive. Value offsets the price.

Coming back to the wire cable customer meeting, I learned another important lesson from this short interaction.

You might mistakenly think that the customer paid the full initially quoted price because the salesperson made a good argument. That was not the case and not the point. The salesperson did not walk away with an agreement at the initially quoted price; he still had to provide a discount. But he walked away with a better price than he would have if he hadn't made the argument!

His argument helped him hold his ground. Without reinforcing value, the negotiation would have deteriorated into a price-cutting game. And without the ability to communicate clear differentiation points, most likely, he would have had to provide an even deeper discount to get the business.

In the example of your used car, finishing the sentence, "My asking price is $2,000 above Kelly Blue Book because this car is worth it, and let me tell you why…" doesn't ensure that you will receive your full asking price. It ensures you get more for your car than if you hadn't made that argument.

Sales managers get frustrated with repeated requests for customer discounts. They tell me that their salespeople are better at negotiating with them than with customers. A salesperson's request to match a competitor's price clearly indicates that negotiating began before the selling process was complete. Price becomes an issue early in a negotiation when the customer doesn't distinguish between the competition and the product and services you offer. Selling on value has a distinct advantage over selling on price.

I'm sure your sales managers will agree that the best sales-people are the best negotiators. Salespeople who genuinely believe in their product or service and the value they bring to their customers will get a better price than those who don't. Lesser-skilled salespeople concede early in the sales process in hopes the other side might bite.

The final lesson from witnessing this wire cable negotiation may be the most valuable of all. The salesperson did not differentiate his product, cable wire, from the competition by talking about its features and benefits. I'm not even sure it is possible to differentiate something sold by the ton and the mile. After all, it's just cable, right?

Instead, he explained how his company provides better post-sales service and in-field support, better response time to emergency orders, better terms and conditions, and better "value-added" services than the competition. He differentiated the company, not the product. He "sold" the value of his company's investments to better serve and support its customers.

Salespeople know that relationships are essential to their success. The mistake they make is to think of customer relationships in terms that are too narrow. This narrows their ability to hold their ground.

Customers have a relationship with the salesperson, of course. But they also have a relationship with the product, service and support organization and the company as a financial entity. So, although your company may have a product that is considered, and in fact may be, a commodity, like wire cable, that doesn't necessarily put you into a commoditized position. If you can differentiate one or all of the relationships the customer has with your company, you can better defend your price.

Salespeople cannot afford to think of their products or company as commodities. When they lose confidence in their products, company, or services they are poorer negotiators. Failure to believe in your company and products plays into customer's hands. They will leverage a late shipment or customer service lapse to get a better deal. They will tell every salesperson from every company that they are "the worst" if it gives them an edge. Good salespeople resist customer attempts to de-value their product offering and put them in a weaker negotiating position. Agreeing with the customer that your price is too high helps no one, especially you.

You can't defend your price if you don't defend your product.

It is much easier to hold your ground when you genuinely believe that your product is worth the money. The Caterpillar people believe their bulldozers are better than John Deere's. Nike people believe their athletic footwear is better than Adidas, and Pacific Life salespeople believe their insurance products and service are better than MetLife. This translates into a significantly higher average selling price because they believe in their products, and no buyer can convince them otherwise. But customers will continue to commoditize, and companies will continue to differentiate, because that's the game.

As for wire cable, it isn't easy to differentiate the product because it is a commodity. But the company worked hard in other areas; service, support, and financing to provide more value to their customers. Investing in those differentiators doesn't necessarily get customers to accept their list price; it allows them to get more for their products than their competitors.

A good salesperson's job is to build the value of their product, service, or company. The customer tries to tear it down. You talk about your value proposition; they complain that your company is hard to do business with. You talk about your product; they talk about the lack of post-service support. Their job is to counter your value proposition with a de-value proposition.

To illustrate my point, let's consider the situation of two people arguing over a generic automobile: a black, four-door Ford Taurus with no extras or additional whistles or bells. As generic and basic a purchase I can think of and an exaggeration, but with a purpose.

The potential buyer says, "This is the most basic car anyone could ever buy." (De-value proposition.)

The seller says, "Yes, they are in pretty high demand." (Value proposition)

The buyer counters, "But they're everywhere. A dime a dozen." (De-value proposition.)

The seller counters, "There is a reason for that: best-selling car of the year." (Value proposition.)

The buyer says, "But it's black, which is the worst color." (De-value proposition.)

The seller says, "Black is the most popular color of any automobile. Just look it up." (Value proposition.)

And the buyer says, "But it has no extras." (De-value proposition.)

To which the seller responds, "Which gives you the ability to add any after-market options. It's totally customizable." (Value proposition.)

This example is unrealistic, but I use it to show how rebuttals are necessary to hold your ground.

First Offers Tactics

FIRST OFFER TACTIC #1
Get them to put the number on the table first.

Regardless of what you may have been told, negotiations don't begin until one side puts a number on the table. Experts will tell you that the preparation before presenting opening offers significantly affects your negotiation outcome, and that is true.

Handling a buyer's initial challenges and resisting their tactics is key to leveling the playing field. It's called positioning and can be useful for them, especially if you fail to recognize it is being used against you. I hear variations of the same statements every week by customers trying to gain a negotiating edge.

"You need us more than we need you" or "You do want our business, don't you?" or "We gave you a lot of business last year, so we are going to want some significant price reductions" are intended to soften you up for the bargaining that follows. A good negotiator identifies and deals with these positioning statements to re-level the playing field right from the start.

When a customer says, "You need us more than we need you," you respond with, "Need is too strong a word. But yes, we would like to reach a mutually beneficial agreement."

When they ask, "You do want our business, don't you?" a good response is, "We want any business that makes sense for both of us." And finally, "We gave you a lot of business last year" should be deflected with "We are pleased to have had you as a customer and feel that we deliver excellent value for the money you spend with our company."

This game seems petty, but it comes with the territory. When customers try to weaken your position, you need to counter-position, especially before discussing price.

Savvy negotiators know that being first to reveal their opening position puts them at a tactical disadvantage. But getting even the savviest negotiators to reveal their opening price is a skill that can be learned pretty quickly. Your most powerful tool is a good question. Here are some that will help.

"Is this a budgeted item? If so, can you share your budget with me?"

"Do you have a number in mind, and if so, can you give me an idea of how much?"

"Can you give me a ballpark figure to begin with?"

"What do you think this is worth?"

"When you bought something similar in the past, how much did you pay?"

There is an art to skilled negotiation. It isn't as simple as asking the other side the question and moving on. When dealing with tough negotiators, you need to persist as they try to keep their cards close to their vest. A worthy opponent will answer a question with a question.

You ask, "What do you think it is worth?" and they reply, "I don't know. What do you think it is worth?"

You ask, "Do you have a price in mind?" and the other side responds with, "Do you have a budget you need to stay within?"

The best response to a negotiator's parroted question is a sophisticated version of "I asked you first!"

They say, "Give me a ballpark price, so I have something to work with." and you respond with, "Can you give me a range you have in mind."

Or they ask, "What do you think it's worth?" You respond with, "I don't know. Did you have an approximate cost target in mind?"

And if they ask, "Do you give a volume discount?" respond with, "How large a volume are we talking about?"

Even more important is being careful and cautious when answering questions from a hardball negotiator, as you can quickly find yourself on the defensive. Take your time and think about the impact of the answer. Tough negotiators don't back off, like in this exchange.

"Does your company ever give 90-day payment terms?"

The salesperson innocently replies, "We don't like to extend the payments out more than 30 days."

The buyer pushes harder, "You said you don't like to, but I asked if you ever do it?"

To this, the salesperson answers, "It has to be a special case."

The buyer pounces, "So you do it, but only in cases that you think warrant special consideration."

"Um... I guess."

You can see where this is going.

Stop and think before responding to questions in any negotiation, but especially when the other side is playing hardball.

Here is an example of why it is so important to be persistent in getting the other side to give you a number.

Some years ago, I worked on a negotiation for a large piece

of reconditioned semiconductor manufacturing equipment. In a preliminary meeting, we asked how much the sellers originally paid for the equipment as we wanted to avoid basing our first offer on the list price when the sellers acquired the equipment. I was pretty sure that in the depressed market of three years earlier, they purchased the equipment at a substantial discount.

Their response was, "We don't believe the original price is relevant to this negotiation. We prefer to focus on how much the equipment is worth today."

When my client capitulated with, "Okay, we understand." I pulled them out of the room for a sidebar.

"We need to find out how much they originally paid for the equipment. The original purchase price is relevant to how much we offer, but it puts them in a weaker negotiating position if they reveal it. Let's apply pressure and see what happens."

We explained that we needed to know the original price before going any further. They reluctantly told us they acquired the equipment at a 20 percent discount. Had my client knuckled under so quickly, the negotiation's starting point would have been substantially higher.

One of the reasons I enjoy the world of negotiation because it forces me to deal with ethical issues. Depending on a person's concept of fairness, they can reach very different negotiation outcomes.

My insurance client is a leader in the wealth management transfer business, life insurance policies that allow for intergenerational wealth transfer with substantially fewer tax penalties. (Life insurance tax liabilities are much less than inheritance taxes) As you can imagine, due to the huge payouts, these policies come with a hefty monthly premium, sometimes hundreds of thousands of dollars per month for a 9-digit payout at the time of death. When designing these insurance strategies, the broker (insurance agent) is given a range of premiums by the insurance company underwriter. Whichever premium the broker quotes within the range will be profitable for the insurance company. The broker almost always has a premium amount in mind, but it is common practice to let the client go first; to have the high-net-worth-individual (HNWI) reveal how large a monthly premium he or she are can afford.

There is a reason for this.

If the HNWI quotes a higher monthly premium than the agent has in mind, it is all gravy. If they give a premium lower, it's a negotiation.

The ethical question arises when the HNWI gives a number significantly higher. The moral question then becomes, "Would you increase your original premium amount, ensuring more profit for yourself and your firm, or would you stick with your original number as a "fair" premium?"

The universal response for insurance companies is to raise the premium even if the original number was "fair."

While it is within the boundaries of typical negotiating, I'm not sure this is fair. This situation doesn't fall into my personal definition of fairness. I believe in fairness and fair play. Getting a better price simply because you can, seems unethical. I prefer to keep my prices fair or at least "defensible." But it is safe to assume hardball negotiators don't feel the same amount of re-morse as win-win players would about raising their price. One top-rated negotiating book title declares, "You don't get what you deserve, you get what you negotiate." In zero-sum negotiations, a "fair" agreement is only fair if the buyer wins.

(Ever hear of something called Stranger Owned Life Insurance, or STOLI? In exchange for a substantial financial incentive at the policy approval, a corporation will pay you for the privilege of insuring your life for millions of dollars. The insurance company receives the multi-million policy payoff when you kick the bucket. It is as close to a sure bet as anything for the insurer, as long as you don't live longer than expected.)

FIRST OFFER TACTIC #2
Make them defend their number.

Once your opponent makes the first offer, challenging them to defend that number puts you on the offensive. Tough buyers are predictable, so assume you are low-balled, and there is plenty of profit margin baked into their first number. Asking them how they arrived at that number is fair. Tough negotiators are seldom prepared for this tactic, and it catches them off guard, especially if they haven't thought it through.

A couple of years ago, I was looking to replace the engine of my Toyota 4-Runner. I loved this SUV, but with more than 200,000 miles, it had lost most of its get-up-and-go. I priced a new factory-built replacement engine from Toyota. The company wanted $4,500 for a brand-new engine. That was more than I was prepared to pay.

By luck, I found one on Craigslist from a local Seattle private party. The ad listed the price of $1,500, a phone number, and a name, Adolph. I called and asked about the engine. He told me that it was in excellent condition and had a local mechanic who would vouch for the engine's condition. It was clear he didn't want to negotiate the price.

"You saw that my price is firm, right?"

"Yes, I noticed that. Do you mind if I ask you a question about the price?"

"You can, but I'm not budging," He said, already getting testy.

"I know, I know. I want a little more information if that's okay with you?"

"Fine, but my price is firm."

"Do you mind sharing with me how you arrived at the price for the engine?"

"Whaddya mean?"

"Well, you seem pretty fixed on the $1,500 for the engine, so I thought you most likely did your homework," I replied.

"It's in good shape, and I haven't seen any others for sale. I figured I could get $1,500 for it."

"So, the $1,500 price is something you came up with on your own."

"Yep, but it doesn't matter. The price is the price; take it or leave it."

"Well, it seems like a lot of money if you can't verify its true market value. Not sure it is worth that much."

Feeling like the sale might be slipping away, Adolph shared more information than he should have.

"To be honest, we're about to move to Texas and I need the money to cover our moving expenses."

In that short statement, Adolph told me two things.

The first and lesser-important revelation is that he is a motivated seller. I assumed most people would not want to drag a used automobile engine from the Northwest to the Southwest if they could avoid it. His second and much more critical revelation was this; Adolph did not know what the engine was worth. He used an arbitrary number based on his moving expenses, and by attempting to protect his first offer with a plea to my good nature, he left himself wide open. It offered me a distinct advantage – and another ethical dilemma.

Let's deal with the distinct advantage first.

Not having a logical explanation of how he arrived at the engine's price, Adolph put himself in a difficult position. Using sympathy as a negotiation tool makes any price tough to defend. If he'd done his homework and knew the factory engine's cost, he would be in a much better place. His defense could have been, "A new engine will cost you $4,500, plus shipping and handling." That would have been a much stronger argument than the sob story about his expensive move to Texas. He would have been in a stronger negotiation position and gotten more for the engine. Or I would have had to fight harder to get him to reduce his price. But without a credible defense of his price, I had the upper hand.

I offered him $700. He took it immediately.

If he had been even a marginally better negotiator, he should have countered my low-ball offer at least once. If he'd given it more thought, he could quickly figure out that my options were limited. His was the only used engine on the market, as far as I could tell.

Now for another ethical dilemma.

When I share my "Adolph" story, people respond in one of two ways.

Half say I paid too much for the engine, even at $700. They argue that because Adolph was in the middle of a move, I could have offered him anything, and he would take it.

I'm not sure about that.

The other half says that because $1,500 is a fair price and Adolph is in a difficult situation, it's unfair to take advantage. They advocate being generous and paying him what he wants.

Depending on which group you fall into, the price you end up paying will be very different. With the first mindset, I could take advantage of Adolph's unfortunate circumstances by offering a rock-bottom price. People with the second and more generous mindset could argue that $1,500 is fair, especially when considering the lack of other options, and I help a guy out of a tough situation.

Regardless of how you view the situation, it's clear that had Adolph been better able to defend his position, I would have paid more for the engine. Adolph's hardball approach worked against him.

Now, the rest of the story.

After closing the deal, I drove to Adolph's to pick up the engine. Once the engine was in my truck, he offered a beer, and we sat for a minute.

I shared with him that I had lived in Texas after graduate school and asked how he was feeling about the move. He said his family is looking forward to moving to a warmer, sunnier climate.

"We are tired of the rain, and my wife's folks live in Dallas."

But then added without really thinking.

"And get this, my employer, General Motors, wrote us a blank check for $25,000 to cover moving expenses. It won't cost me half that much, so I'm taking my family on a cruise with the rest."

Something tells me that if I had paid his full asking price, he would have never mentioned General Motors' check. Obviously, Adolph didn't remember using the sob story to get me to pay $1,500 for the engine.

The Adolph story raises the thorny question of whether you negotiate the best deal possible for your side regardless of the carnage you leave in your wake, or do you negotiate a deal that is "fair." It is a fair question.

Just because you know how to play hardball doesn't mean you should. I don't negotiate at flea markets or craft fairs because I know these people have families to feed and bills to pay. It doesn't seem fair to grind them down to save a bit of money. When I buy from local vendors, I never haggle because my community benefits when they benefit.

But when it comes to people playing hardball, I feel little remorse for getting a deal that favors my interests over theirs. Like I learned from Adolph (after the fact), it is hard to know whether someone is playing win-win and revealing his interests to you or playing zero-sum and bending the truth to get a profitable deal. There are many negotiations in which the other side seems cooperative and friendly when they are actually using the relationship to get concessions.

Last year I went with a friend to a "no-haggle" car dealership to familiarize myself with their approach. The salesperson was friendly, the sales manager was friendly, and even the finance guy seemed friendly until we went to sign the final documents. Before providing the final papers, the finance person pulled out an extended warranty using this last-minute tactic to pressure my friend into buying coverage he didn't want or need.

But when I counseled him to turn it down, the finance manager insisted he needed a signature on the warranty declining the coverage. I told the finance manager that he would have to do it without any signature if he wanted the deal. Realizing this was a dealbreaker, he quickly backed down.

When it comes to honesty, I stick to tactics I feel are fair, whether in a win-win or zero-sum negotiation. Getting the other side to defend their price is an acceptable tactic either way. As with Adolph, having a couple of simple, useful questions can change the outcome significantly. I typically use versions of the following questions to test the other side.

"How did you come up with that number?"

"Why did you start with such a low/high number?"

"How did you arrive at that?"

"I don't understand your reasoning. Can you help me by explaining how you came up with it?"

"That number seems like a lot to ask for; can you tell me what you based it on?"

Using questions to force the other side to step back and defend their price, weakens their opening position, and strengthens yours.

I've heard some less-than-useful responses over the years, like "I just feel it is worth that much," or "I still owe money on it," and "I knew you were going to start high, so I started low."

To soften up zero-sum negotiators even more, ask about flexibility. Tough negotiators always position their number as "firm." But you can get a sense of the negotiator's flexibility by asking:

"How firm are these prices/terms/conditions?"

"Do you have any room to move? In which areas: price, terms, or conditions?"

"Are these numbers firm or negotiable?"

If you get them to answer any of those questions, remember:

"Negotiable" means they have some room to maneuver. "Or Best Offer" (OBO) means they have a lot. And "firm" doesn't mean they have no room to maneuver, it means you will have to work harder to wring out any concession.

Sales managers may appreciate this next couple of points.

Some salespeople tell me that their job doesn't require negotiation, even when it does. They insist they don't have input into customer prices because they are negotiated at a national level by higher-ups in the organization.

That may be true, but even if your price is fixed, other things are not. Sample products, terms and conditions, delivery, training, and guaranteed usage quantities can all be negotiated. Tough customers want their "pound of flesh" and don't measure "flesh" solely in dollars and cents. Expect them to put as many things into play as possible: shipping, sampling, financing, etc. A negotiator who needs a one-of-a-kind product and has little pricing leverage will push for other concessions. They will pay your higher price but cherry-pick other things to improve their side of the bargain.

I was in my investment counselor's office some months back talking about assets. I had an investment with another brokerage house that was providing less than stellar returns. I asked him about moving it into one of his firm's funds with higher potential. He thought it was a good idea, so we completed the fund's transfer for a substantial amount of money.

After completing the paperwork, I jokingly said, "When my father was young, if he moved that much money into an investment, they would have given him something as a thank you."

My broker laughed and said, "Sure, like a toaster or something."

"Right," I replied, now only half-joking, "like a toaster."

"We haven't given out toasters in a long time." the broker said with good-natured sarcasm.

"I know. But you must have something to give clients in return for their business. You and your firm get up-front fees and commissions. All I get is a return when and if the fund does well. But how about something now?"

"You're not serious?" He looked incredulous.

"Even if it is some promotional item or something, you know... for the effort," doing my best Bill Murray.

He mumbled and opened his desk drawer, which was crammed with golf balls, pens, leather binders, and all kinds of paraphernalia.

"You mean stuff like this?" he asked.

"Exactly!" I said.

He handed over several nice pen and pencil sets, a couple of sleeves of golf balls, and two leather binders.

"Don't the investment houses make these things for you to give clients?"

"No one ever asks."

"I think if someone gives your firm this much money, they should at least get a pen."

We had a good laugh, and my daughters got some very expensive school supplies. My tactics might seem petty to some, but the lesson is that if you're in the position to offer the customer anything; terms, conditions, after-sales service and support, or even a pen and pencil set, you do negotiate.

Good salespeople are always negotiating.

The second point has to do with decision making authority and negotiation. Salespeople often tell me that when they don't have enough authority to finalize a deal it puts them in a weak negotiating position. There are two legitimate sides to this argument.

Buying yourself time by deflecting to management approval is sometimes a useful tactic. Taking time to strategize before responding to a customer is valuable in the right situation.

However, there are situations in which it is not in the salesperson's best interest to have the power to finalize a deal. Having the authority may give you more negotiating freedom, but it can also be more responsibility than you want. Sometimes, management should make those critical decisions. In hospital/insurer negotiations, executives rarely get involved until the end of the negotiation. This is because the most critical and difficult decisions are typically left until last. Upper management gets involved to protect their contract negotiators from the consequences of making a poor decision that might jeopardize both the deal and the negotiator's career.

Telling a customer, "This is the best price my manager will allow me to give you," as a ploy to evade the back-and-forth erodes your negotiating power if the timing isn't right. Even if it's true that management holds the ultimate negotiating power, you want the person sitting across the table to think you are the heavy, the muscle. You create a more powerful negotiation position by making a case for your product's value, not by deflecting to your manager. Positioning value communicates not just value but authority as well. "Our prices are fair and reasonable, and let me tell you why…" conveys to buyers that they need to negotiate with you before getting any concession, even if that concession is escalating the negotiation to your manager's level.

If you spend enough time in my profession, you run into people who think they are talented negotiators but aren't. A couple of year ago, I competed with another negotiation expert to create a seminar for a client. In a clumsy attempt to get a better price, the Sales V.P. told me, "Your competition really wants my business. They are aggressively discounting their fees to win the contract."

Then in an even more amateur attempt, he added, "They told me they would do whatever it takes. He repeated for emphasis, "Whatever it takes."

After thinking it through, I asked quizzically, "Do you think this guy can make your salespeople better negotiators when he's already told you that he will do anything to get your business?"

The V.P. thought for a minute.

"Oh yeah. I don't think he would."

First Offer Tactic #3
Conditionally put your number on the table.

At some point, you have to provide the other side something to work with. Positioning your first counteroffer (remember, the other side made the first offer) as conditional helps you avoid being trapped in a corner. Using a phrase like, "We feel that our offer is fair and reasonable; however, if you want to discuss other possible ways to reach agreement, we are open to that," positions your approach as firm but negotiable. But be prepared for challenges. How will you respond if your opponent asks how you came up with your offer? How will you respond if the other side asks if your price flexibility? How will you respond to the question, "How firm is your price? The wrong answer is "Firm," but so is the answer, "Negotiable."

After uncovering and challenging their number, you can better determine whether your opening price is too high or too low and adjust your strategy accordingly. If the other side has a weak argument for their opening position, it can allow you to ask for more or offer less.

Before providing an opening price, there are a couple of things to think about. One is how much the customer values your products or services. Some value is tangible and can be quantified, like price and financing, etc. But intangibles have a value as well. Quality, company stability, market share, and customer service all contribute value to the customer relationship. The value your customer puts in your product or service an important indicator of your negotiation leverage. If you have a highly differentiated product or service with a few or a limited number of competitors, it gives you substantial leverage, especially if the customer buys into your value proposition.

FIRST OFFER TACTIC #4
Defend your price.

Once your number is on the table, defending it is critical to reaching better agreements. Without a concrete explanation for the reasons behind his price for the engine, Adolph was immediately on the defensive.

Suppose Adolph responded to my challenge by saying, "The retail price of a new engine of $4,500. But because I want to make a quick sale, and this one has 10,000 miles, I decided $1,500 was a fair and reasonable price." I would have been on the defensive immediately.

But he didn't, so I wasn't.

Let's consider defending your price from the customer's perspective. The only way for the customer to close the gap between the higher price you want to charge them and the lower price they want to pay is to either convince you that your product isn't worth the difference or get you to make concessions until you reach the amount they are willing to pay. The other side's job is to convince you, the seller, that your product is a commodity. If they can convince you that your product is no different from your competition, you have less leverage. Yet, I watch salespeople let buyers commoditize their product or service without putting up a fight.

A couple of years ago, the Purchasing Department at Caterpillar Tractor contacted me to discuss my contract renewal for the upcoming year. The department had an issue with the wording of my standard contract. I include a 30-day cancellation clause in all my contracts to protect me from last-minute shifts in client priorities and interruptions in my cash flow. CAT asked me to remove the clause from my current contract.

I asked why it was an issue, as all my previous contracts contained the clause. The contract negotiator replied, "We are expecting a tough year in the housing market, so we need to reduce our financial exposure wherever possible." I agreed that risk management is important but stated that I wanted to explain my side of the dilemma.

"Suppose a customer agrees to buy a bulldozer and at the last minute cancels the order. What does CAT do in that situation?"

"We certainly don't make the customer pay for the machine if that's what you mean."

"Yes, but what happens to the bulldozer? Do you sell it to someone else?"

"We put it back in the storage lot until someone else wants to buy it."

"Precisely my point." I said, "My services are different. When you cancel my business at the last minute, I don't have a 'bulldozer' to sell to someone else. I can rarely find another client to fill that open training day on such short notice."

Frustrated, the accounting person said, "All I know is that you are the only consultant who has a cancellation clause in the contract. We need consistency."

What would you do next? Would you accept the argument and eliminate the clause or refuse and risk losing a valuable customer?

My response is not one typically heard by "buyers" in a customer negotiation.

"With all due respect, the services I offer are different from other consultants, and let me tell you why..." By now, you should know where this goes. In the end, I was able to keep the clause in my contract for another year.

But by using this tactic, I risked the client saying, "Well, we will just use other consultants then." To mitigate this risk, I had to convince the purchasing person that my value was substantial enough to allow the clause as an "exception." Buyers sometimes aren't aware they're trying to commoditize your offering; they are just making an argument to justify their position.

It gives them an edge. Your job is to make the argument that your product or service is different and better.

Do not give up your opening price without a good fight. Tough negotiators will make you and your products "the worst" to increase their leverage. They'll complain about your product, your service, and your price, using whatever it takes to get an edge. They will debunk even the most valid value arguments.

Don't take it personally; it's their job. Your job is to argue that yours is a differentiated, high quality, and valuable product. They position problems, you position benefits; they position similarities, you position uniqueness. Look them in the eye and defend your product, service, and price. Your profitability depends on the quality and confidence of your argument. Sell your value before making any concessions.

It would be nice to have a truly unique, highly differentiated product, so you have the upper hand in a negotiation. But salespeople tell me all the time, "My product is a commodity. My company doesn't differentiate our products, services, or any other aspect that might add value to our clients. That is why we don't have any negotiation leverage."

There are companies whose offering is generic with little ability to differentiate. But realize that a strong, differentiated product is not the only arrow in your quiver. Even if you have a me-too product, you can still reach satisfactory agreements; you just need to be very good at trading concessions.

You Are a Better Negotiator Already

Here is a situation I found myself in some years ago. Based on what you've learned so far, try to figure out how you might approach this negotiation differently.

On a recent Friday afternoon, I returned from working on the east coast. I had a workshop with a local Seattle company scheduled for Monday morning and needed copies of the materials that accompany the class. In my line of work, you make many copies: copies of training workbooks, copies of project planners, copies of client materials. Not far from my house is a copy center. I use it regularly because it's close and convenient.

On my way back from the airport, I stopped at FedEx Office (Ex-Kinko's) with the workbook master document and requested 50 copies by Sunday afternoon. The counter person informed me that it was impossible to meet my deadline because of the heavy workload and lack of staff. I asked about alternatives.

The clerk told me the FedEx Office University store could meet my printing deadline because they had the large staff required by University of Washington students. Their customer base, students, typically do things at the last minute. Reluctant to drive to the University district (10 miles, 20 minutes), I asked that the clerk call and make sure they could meet my deadline. He did and assured me the copies would be ready by Sunday morning if I could deliver the master copy by that afternoon.

I drove the distance and dropped off the documents.

On Sunday morning, I returned to the University FedEx Store and handed the clerk my job ticket. He put the boxes of materials on the counter and presented me with a bill for $500, and as is my usual routine, I asked if he might give me a volume discount.

"I'm not sure, but this seems like a larger order than is typical for FedEx. Is that right?" I asked.

The clerk replied, "Yes, especially in this store. U.W. students usually get one or two copies."

"Can you do something for me on the price?"

Confused, the clerk asked what I meant.

"I do a lot of business with FedEx Office, and I was wondering if I can get a discount for such a big order?"

The clerk left and returned in a minute with Greg, the store manager. He asked how he could help. I amicably explained my situation and reiterated my request for a discount.

Greg smiled and replied, "I think we can do something since you are such a good customer. How about 20-percent off?"

"Great!"

He knocked $100 off the invoice and gave me my box of materials.

Why did Greg give me a $100 discount? Perhaps he thought I would repay his good deed with loyalty and bring more work to his store. But as a small business owner who often has to produce workbooks on short notice while keeping a sharp eye on the bottom line, my loyalty is often based on how much it costs to run my business. Giving such a steep discount in exchange for goodwill is not usually a sound negotiation strategy — at least not with me.

Who has the leverage in this situation? Greg, or me? Greg had the materials; I needed the materials. I was on one side of the counter without my materials; he was on the other with his hand on my materials.

Greg was in the more powerful position, but instead of using that power, he capitulated, providing me a significant discount and earning significantly less profit for his store. To be fair, Greg is a store manager and not a professional negotiator, and most people probably don't ask for a discount at a copy store. Likely, Greg doesn't get much negotiating experience. Another factor influencing amateur and professional negotiators alike is whether they are negotiating with their money. In this situation, Greg wasn't, and I was. He was negotiating with FedEx's money and personally had little to lose. His performance is likely based on customer satisfaction, not profit margin. If Greg was compensated on profitability, I doubt he would have been so generous.

Now, put yourself in the same position as Greg. I come into your store to pick up my print job and ask if you can provide me a discount on such a large job. What would be a better response than "Sure, how about 20 percent?"

How would you respond?

The question, "How much of a discount did you have in mind?" would have immediately changed the dynamics.

I might ask for a 20-percent discount, and your counter of 10 percent would net you $50 more profit. Another improved response would be to negotiate a volume discount based on future purchases. Greg could have promised a discount on the next copy job and give me his business card with the deal written on it.

Greg did not negotiate; he capitulated.

Here's the rest of the story.

Two weeks later, I found myself in a similar situation, needing a quick turnaround on workshop materials late in the week. Anticipating the problem with the previous job, I made a point of getting the materials to my local FedEx (not the University, the store down the street) on Thursday, not Friday. The clerk said my printing would be ready Sunday.

I returned to pick up my materials, and when presented with the bill, said to the clerk, "When I use the University FedEx Office, Greg, the manager there, gives me a 20-percent discount on big orders." Without flinching, the clerk calculated a 20 percent discount and revised my bill. A successful transaction completed — at least, successful on my end.

Some might see my tactic as unethical and unfair, but that is too thorny an issue to discuss at this point. This story reinforces the idea that poor negotiators give ground too quickly and get nothing in return. Greg gave me $100 directly from his bottom line and received nothing in return: no loyalty, no promise of business, nothing but my "thanks." I give him credit for being a nice guy, but he could still be a nice guy and get more for his $100.

The Rocky Story

SLIPPING LEVERAGE

O ne thing I hate to do is show my hand, but I had no choice.

If I didn't call the pet store soon, the dog might be sold. I needed something to work with, like a price for ... Rocky. The owner would know I was interested, so I decided to ask the price of a couple of dogs to throw him off the scent. That might save me from losing more leverage. But let's face it; the fact I was calling weaken my leverage.

First, I checked the web.

Wheaten Terriers; good with kids . . . check; grow to about 50 pounds . . . check; are not known for digging or chewing up furniture . . . check; are hypoallergenic, they don't shed... check. Not a bad choice for a pet.

Not many Wheatens in or around Seattle, only a couple of adult dogs in the area for sale or adoption. Found a Spokane breeder with Wheaten puppies selling for between $600 and $800. That would cost me a four-hour drive no doubt with an unhappy tweener in the back seat.

None were viable options, but they gave me something to start with, at least.

I called; the owner answered.

"Can I help you?"

"Hi, I'm the guy who came into the store this morning with my daughter looking at your dogs."

"Sorry, we get lots of kids in here every day with their folks." So, this is how it was going to be.

"You might remember my daughter. You showed her the Wheaten terrier."

"Oh yeah, yeah. I remember now. They looked adorable together, a great dog. You interested?"

"We're still exploring options, but I want to know how much you want for the Wheaten and the Standard Poodle."

"Did you have a number in mind? Do you have a budget or something? I can make almost anything work if you want the dog, even payments."

He was answering a question with a question again.

"We want to spend as little as possible. How much do you want for each?"

"The poodle is a good second choice. Not that much fun for children; smart dogs but not a "kid's" dog, if you know what I mean."

"Okay, okay. What about the Wheaten?"

"Do you know much about Wheatens?"

"I did some checking on the web and found out quite a lot."

Poof! A little more leverage up in smoke.

"So, you know they don't shed and are great with kids."

"Yes, but we haven't decided yet. I am just shopping price."

"Okay, well, if you are serious, I can let you have the Wheaten for $1,200."

Caught off guard, I made my first mistake.

"Wow, that's a lot! I can get the same dog from a breeder in Spokane for half that."

And with that, this negotiation began. Both our numbers were on the table, and now it was a matter of reaching a price we could both live with. But with a gap of $600 between us, there was a long way to go.

His next words sent a negotiation shiver up my spine.

"This dog is worth $1,200, and let me tell you why . . ."

The first step in any negotiation is defending your price, and I was sure this guy had a persuasive argument. People negotiating with their own money usually do.

He went on. "My name is Ralph, and you are . . .?"

"Steve . . . Steve Reilly."

"Nice to meet you, Steve."

"First off, Steve. You don't want to drive all the way to Spokane with the idea of getting a dog. What happens if you don't find one that's right for you? I wouldn't take for granted that you'll come back with a dog. Then where will you be?"

"No problem, my business takes me to Spokane all the time."

Okay, my business took me to Spokane once . . . in 2009. Technically, I wasn't lying. Technically.

"Let's say you drive to Spokane and find one. That's great, but what if something's wrong with the dog? What if it's sick or has some genetic problem? A lot of unethical breeders take risks by breeding them too close. Then what do you do, return the dog?"

"That's a point, but I still haven't decided on a Wheaten. And I'm still surprised that your price is double the breeder's."

"For this dog and everything else, $1,200 is an excellent price."

I couldn't help myself . . . I bit. "What do you mean, 'everything else?'"

"For one, we guarantee our dog's health. They're all dewormed, vaccinated, and microchipped in case someone tries to steal him."

This was going to be tougher than I thought . . . and he was just getting started.

"We have an agreement with the local vet for 35 percent off your first visit. If there is anything wrong, we pay the doctor's bill. If there a genetic issue, we refund your money, no questions asked."

He barely took a breath.

"One more thing. I figure you live in the neighborhood. If you kennel your dog here, he will know my staff and me. And if anything goes wrong with the dog, you won't have to go to Spokane to wring someone's neck."

And then . . . dead air.

Ralph shut up and didn't say another word . . . nothing but silence from his end of the phone line. And in that silent gap, I heard a little voice in the back of my head say to me, "Your move, Steve."

After a pause, I used one of my most effective negotiation techniques.

"I'll get back to you," I said . . . and hung up.

Chapter 2

Counteroffer Strategy and Tactics

The customer wanted my client's technology: a new and sophisticated microchip testing process that included software, hardware, post-sale service, and support packages. Their technology reduced downtime and manufacturing costs. But despite a clear and measurable value to the customer and competitive advantage, the salesperson caved.

"Your product is expensive, but I might get my people to commit if you can discount an additional 20 percent. Can you do that?" asked the customer.

"I'm not allowed to discount this product, but how about if we split the cost of the installation? Would that help?"

"Maybe," the customer responded. "But I'll have to talk to my team and get back to you."

I butted in. "If you don't mind, can I ask a question regarding your decision-making process?"

"Uh, sure," she said, looking a bit confused as I was along for a field ride, not a representative of his company.

"You said earlier that this technology provides a significant advantage over your current semiconductor test methodology. Is that right?"

"Yes, the benchmark testing showed improved efficiency and higher throughput," she said hesitantly, not knowing where I might be going with this line of questioning.

"You also said it brings quantitative value to you and your company. Am I correct?"

"Yes, our numbers show a reduction in errors and longer uptime for the fabrication process."

"Are the other decision-makers aware of the improvement in MTBF [Mean Time Between Failures) and that impact of savings and efficiencies gained by my client's products?" I asked.

I sensed her apprehension building, "So I expect you want us to pay for the entire installation instead of splitting the costs with your client?"

"No, not at all. I am asking if you can have the evaluation completed by the end of the month in return for absorbing half of the installation costs?"

"That seems reasonable."

"Then we have a deal?"

"We have a deal."

Counteroffer Strategy

The all-too-common belief that conceding in a negotiation weakens your power is not always the case. Being too rigid and inflexible can cost you in a negotiation, while a well-thought-out concession strategy can get you more than refusing to negotiate.

There are clear differences between win-win and zero-sum approaches when making concessions. In a win-win approach, both parties openly share their interests in a noble attempt to collaboratively "problem solve." Once interests are on the table, the parties create mutually agreeable solutions to satisfy their interests.

William Ury uses a story of two men arguing in a library. The librarian comes over and asks if she can help. One man says he wants the window open, while the other wants it closed. The librarian asks them why they want what they want. One wants the window open for the fresh air while the other wants it closed because it blows his papers off the desk. As Ury tells it, the librarian thinks about it for a moment and then opens a window on the other side of the room, which satisfies both parties.

The moral of the story is that a compromise of a half-open window would not have satisfied either party and that knowing the motivation behind the demands enables parties to reach a more mutually acceptable and creative agreement. It's a nice little story that teaches a key point regarding the win-win approach. But if you apply the same scenario to a typical hardball situation, one side doesn't care what or why the other person wants what he wants. He just wants the damn window closed!

Win-win may be appealing, but it's not a very effective approach when the other side tries to get as much as possible. Keeping your cards close to the vest is smart, while putting your interests on the table invites the other side to take advantage.

I have two retail clients in Seattle. Both focus on strong service, great products, and customer loyalty. The managers of their sourcing groups wanted their buyers to become better negotiators; they needed help reaching better agreements with suppliers.

It so happened that both clients used the same offshore supplier for basic materials, a Korean fabric manufacturer. It is common for specialty fabrics to have a limited number of suppliers in this industry. By chance, I had the opportunity to see both companies pricing for the same fabric at the same volumes. One was paying a 30-percent premium over the other manufacturer's price. The lower price client used a firm but fair approach with all suppliers; they negotiated from a cautious and strong position. Their purchasing focused on the business relationship's benefit to their company's specific costs and delivery needs.

The client paying the higher price valued its "relationship" treating suppliers as "partners" in the business. This approach would have been all well and good had the supplier been playing the same game, which they weren't.

Additionally, the Korean supplier often shipped orders earlier than the agreed-upon delivery date to create additional inventory space. Though it was inconvenient and changed the supply chain metrics, the retailer agreed to accommodate the request as a goodwill gesture. The client paying the lower price for the fabric also accepted early shipments from the supplier but only in return for an additional 2 percent discount as an early stocking fee.

To my amazement, even after pointing out the price difference, the retailer continued to pay the higher price. It believed the advantages outweigh the disadvantages and making allowances in the name of collaboration is worth the premium. On the other hand, the retailer with a lower price hasn't seen any erosion of loyalty or service based on a stronger negotiation position. They continue to enjoy lower sourcing costs and excellent service.

Which raises the question, "Should I make concessions in return for goodwill?"

The core idea behind win-win negotiating is that people are good, and when given a chance, will reciprocate. All too often, salespeople make concessions with some vague notion they will benefit in the long run and that having "goodwill" might, just might, make the other side play nice. This philosophy is noble, but it is not a negotiation strategy.

Goodwill is nice to have, but don't count on it having any lasting value from a zero-sum negotiator. Promises without any intention of delivering are common. "C'mon, buddy. I'll give you first shot at future business if you cut me a deal here" is often forgotten or ignored. When dealing with tough negotiators, only a clear agreement on reciprocal value is acceptable: shipping charges for payment terms; post-sale service for additional volume.

I also discourage "goodwill" concessions in win-win situations.

Remember Adolph's sob story about moving expenses. He wasn't in a tough financial position, but he played it that way in a bid to use my goodwill for some extra money.

It isn't always smart to deny a customer's request but integrating the concept of a "fair trade" into goodwill concessions is a good idea no matter the negotiator's' approach.

To develop an effective strategy in this second negotiation phase, it is critical to figure out the answer to the two following questions, "How much do I concede?" and "How much do I ask for in return?"

The answer to the first question is about how much ground you give on your first counter. If you can quantify your concession's value, you can ask for something similar in return.

You want to avoid setting a bad precedent. Too much distance between your first offer and your first counter can damage trust and encourages the other side to be less accommodating. The amount of ground you give should be "reasonable." Conceding less than 1 percent in value seems unreasonable. Still, a more-than-20-percent concession sends the message you were trying to take advantage with your first offer. A conservative concession with specific and measurable reciprocal concessions is the best choice with a tough customer.

I have two Seattle clients with very different negotiation styles.

One makes software for the gaming market and their buyers are fair but tough. When I quote this client for a piece of work, they always come back to negotiate a lower price... always. Knowing their style impacts how I price my services to them. I give myself enough room to maneuver, so I have ground to give; I leave a bigger cushion.

My other client is a retailer whose buyers prefer not to deliver bad news. If my pricing is outside their parameters, they give the business to another vendor, then go "radio-silent." Their non-confrontational approach impacts my pricing and approach. I give myself less room to maneuver, a thinner cushion, and try to leave the door open for negotiations by adding, "If my pricing is outside of your parameters, I am happy to discuss options you may not have considered."

Knowing the difference between the company's "style" impacts which game I play. Salespeople who deal with regular, repeat customers have the advantage of getting a feel for their approaches.

The next question to address is, "How much do I ask for in return?"

When leading the *NTY* workshop, participants repeatedly asked for guidance when considering the pricing of concessions. Once again, our canned answer, "Win-win negotiation is about the back-and-forth sharing of interests and possible solutions, not offers and counteroffers," failed to provide any true guidance. (The term counteroffer isn't even mentioned in the original *Getting to Yes* book.)

It is a difficult question. If you concede the cost of better payment terms, how much should you ask for in return? How much is covering shipping costs worth? How much is post-sales training and support worth?

These questions can have a large impact on the profitability of a deal.

Some value is quantifiable. An extended warranty or better payment terms correlates directly to savings or revenue. Accounting departments can calculate the true costs of different financing options or extended payments. When this is the case, your goal should be to cover your costs at least.

However, in some situations there isn't always a straightforward calculation because prices/value are relative.

One good example is the Caterpillar (CAT) "extra bucket dilemma." Among a myriad of products, CAT manufactures and sells high-quality backhoes to the construction industry. For those unfamiliar, a backhoe is a machine with a bucket used to scoop large amounts of dirt and debris into the back of a dump truck or out of the way. The "hoe" part is in the back, thus the name.

It is common for customers to ask the CAT dealership to "throw" an extra detachable bucket into the deal when buying a new backhoe. These machines get a lot of day-to-day wear, and a "tooth" can break unexpectedly. When that happens, workers are left standing around (and being paid) while waiting for the new bucket. That gets expensive. So, the question of how much you ask for in return is important.

But before guessing how much an "extra bucket" is worth, consider these facts. The full retail price of a bucket is $1,500, the manufacturing cost is $500, and the average price of a used bucket available from many sources is $800. And, of course, the customer wants the extra bucket for "free." These factors make the value of the extra bucket relative.

Let me explain the "relative" part.

The CAT salespeople, referred to as "Big Iron" reps, want to recover the bucket's cost at least, right? But a bucket's value depends on which number you use; manufacturing cost, new retail, or used. So, even though asking for something of equivalent "value" might seem straightforward, it is not always so. And when you consider that a CAT backhoe sells for $150,000, the extra bucket is a small part of a larger deal. Refusing to throw in a "free bucket" might cost the company a $150,000 sale.

So, the answer in this case to "How much do I ask for in return?" is "As much as you can!"

In other words, the value of this concession needs to be negotiated.

Counteroffer Tactics

COUNTEROFFER TACTIC #1
Hard sell each concession.

This exchange illustrates the problem with being too "win-win."

My client was in a poor position relative to the competition while trying to close the deal. The industry was price-sensitive with a high inelasticity of demand. (Remember that from your college economics? It means the customer is more likely to buy from someone else if the price increases.) Without much leeway on pricing, the salesperson had the flexibility of providing other value-added services. At this point in the negotiation, he threw everything, including the kitchen sink into the deal.

"If I throw in the warranty and installation services for free, would that get me the business?" His approach was desperate, but the customer didn't mind.

"Maybe," said the customer. "Can you sweeten the deal by throwing in the shipping too? It's not expensive, so you can probably include that, too, right?"

"If I give you a 20-percent discount off the list price, with the warranty, installation, and free shipping, then can we close the deal?"

"Let me run this up the flag-pole and see what my managers say. I'll get back to you."

"Uh, okay. I'll wait for your call. Thanks."

Giving up this much ground is bad negotiating, but the first mistake the salesperson made was acting as if his concessions were "no big deal." The salesperson built little to no value because he failed to "sell" his concessions. Telling the customer his company would provide the items "free of charge" is a mistake and especially costly when dealing with a tough buyer. It is more than just a question of semantics. It is important that when you make a concession, you make it "feel" like a concession to the other side.

When customers get the impression that concessions don't cost the seller much, they don't feel like they are getting much. I've seen salespeople make repeated concessions without the buyer feeling the other side moved much at all. Making a big deal about concessions is a vital part of holding the line against tough bargainers.

Let's start with the word "free."

This goes for every salesperson in every industry in every situation; never use that word, especially when dealing with tough negotiators. Everything you give up has a cost; nothing is ever "no problem," and every concession should be traded for something.

Your company may provide post-sale service and support without charging the customer, but that doesn't mean it is "free." Your company is absorbing the costs for these services, whether the customer pays for them or not.

You and your entire sales organization should immediately change the phrase "We provide that free of charge" to "Our company absorbs the costs."

The new "free" becomes "absorb the cost."

Other ways to say it, "Our company absorbs the costs of these valuable services as part of the value we provide to our customers" or "We pay for these services, so you don't have to." There are many ways to say it and avoid using the words "for free."

Holding your ground means intentionally positioning the value you bring as a defense against discounting. Companies spend money to create support and services to increase the value of their products to the customer. Salespeople should recoup or at least use these "value-adds" to defend their price. A sales manager once told me jokingly that value-adds are things salespeople "value" and "add" cost to the sale.

This may seem petty, but to understand why this is not just a matter of word choice, see how it changes the following scenario dynamics.

The salesperson says, "So you are asking my company to absorb the costs of the installation and warranty. Did I get that right?"

"That's right. You want our business, don't you?"

"We want anyone's business as long as it makes sense to our company."

"Can you do that for me?"

"We've already absorbed a 10 percent discount, and now you're asking us to absorb the costs of installation and warranty as well?"

"Well, how about just the warranty then?" asks the customer.

"I might be able to get my company to go for that, but only if we can get this deal done before the end of the month. Can you do that for me?

By changing the added-value items of warranty and installation costs from "for free" to "absorbed costs," the salesperson increases the value of his offering, which results in the customer reducing his requests for "freebies." It is a simple and very effective technique.

The harder you sell your concessions, the tougher it becomes for the other side to push. Consider this situation. I ask a salesperson for a lower price, and he or she tells me, "I'll talk to my manager and see what I can do." Then the salesperson comes back later and tells me, "I tried, but my manager wouldn't go for it." Of course, I will be disappointed (which I would play for some other concession. See how this goes?).

However, if I ask for a lower price and the salesperson instead responds with, "We don't usually discount this product. But because of your willingness to be reasonable, I will talk to my management and see if the company is willing to absorb these additional costs. Can you give me something to help persuade them? Can you give me something to trade?"

I won't feel so bad when you come back and tell me, "I pulled some strings and convinced my manager to play ball because you are such an important customer. At first, he wanted to pull the deal off the table, but I convinced him to absorb the costs of a two-percent discount in return for a small increase in the parts and labor."

It sounds corny, but it is better than telling a tough customer, "No problem, we can do that." and losing valuable ground or denying a concession because your manager won't let you. Position every concession as a potential deal-breaker against difficult buyers. A good negotiator makes his or her opponent work for everything.

Even if the concession is a long shot, don't be afraid to initiate the request for a concession to throw the other side off balance.

I worked with a software design firm that always requests exclusivity at the beginning of negotiations. They rarely get it but always ask for it. Then they used the denial from the customer as a leverage point in the negotiation.

"We could have given you that price if we had exclusive rights. But since you can't give that to us, we will have to say no to your request."

These responses may sound like lies, but they seem fair against a tough negotiator. Which raises another common question regarding negotiation, "Is it acceptable to lie in a negotiation?"

As a fellow salesperson, I would say no. But flip the question, "Do customers lie to salespeople to get a better deal?" Uh, yes. Many buyers considered stretching the truth or flat-out lying acceptable, especially when dealing with salespeople. The end justifies the means.

This ethical double-talk has a rationale behind it. Most salespeople and their companies are in business for the long term and understand the negative impact deception can have on credibility and trust. Lying in a negotiation is damaging to a long-term, win-win relationship. Hardball negotiators don't share the same concern; they see products as commodities and agreements as transactions.

Treating you and your company as "vendors," they believe or pretend to believe the relationship is inconsequential. For them, lying is simply a way to increase leverage.

I cannot give a definitive answer to whether lying is an acceptable tactic or not. Even some highly ethical negotiators find exaggerating the facts acceptable. Do you really tell a car dealer how much you have to spend, or do you "fudge" a little? Do you really start with your actual budget for a house, or do you give yourself room to maneuver?

Without being moralistic about it, let's leave it at this; the more important a relationship is to you, the less you should lie. But that applies to more than negotiation.

TRADING CONCESSIONS TACTIC #2
Never concede without getting something in return.

Customers, especially tough customers, expect to get concessions without giving any ground. And to be honest, salespeople teach them to expect this by repeatedly conceding without demanding reciprocity.

Before conceding, ask yourself three questions. First, "Do I have to make this concession at all?" Salespeople often believe they are in a less-powerful position because they need to sell something. But if the customer lacks options other than your product, you may be in a more powerful position than you think.

Tough negotiators make idle threats all the time. Threatening to give the business to a competitor gives them leverage, even when it is not an option. If you can determine how serious the customer is about denying you the business, you may have enough leverage to refuse their demand.

The second question is, "Can I make a smaller concession?" If the customer asks for a 5-percent discount, can you offer 2 percent or 3 percent? If they ask for free shipping, can you ask to split the shipping costs? Never take a demand at face value; take it as an opening position. The other side can always refuse. And if they do, at least you set a precedent for future concession requests.

The third, most important, and often neglected question is: "What do I ask for in return?" The key to ensuring your most profitable outcome is setting the expectation that you will not give up something that has a financial impact on your organization without demanding something in return.

Let me illustrate by using a typical negotiation dialogue.

The customer says to you, "Well, I think we can complete this deal if you can get us another 5-percent discount."

Wrong response: "Sure, we can do that."

Another wrong response: "My manager won't let me do that."

Still another wrong response: "Guess I won't make my quota this month."

A better response: "We are cutting our profit margin pretty thin already. But if we can close this deal today, I can convince my company to absorb the cost of a 2-percent discount, but only if we can get the purchase order opened today."

A much better response: "You're killing me here! Our margins are already cut to the bone. I will tell you what I am going to do. If we can close this deal today and get the purchase order opened, I will absorb a 1.75-percent discount on the up-front costs if you are willing to cover the shipping charges. How does that sound?"

Becoming a better negotiator means getting good at playing their game.

TRADING CONCESSION TACTIC #3
Trade the things that cost you the least and have the most value for the other side.

I recently spent a day working with a new client, a major insurance company in Nebraska. After strategizing in a conference room for most of the day, we decided a nice dinner would be a good end to our workday. At the customer's recommendation, we ended up at an expensive local steak house.

After the meal, as the waiter placed the check on the table, my client asked me coyly, "How about we negotiate who pays for dinner?"

He was feeling confident after spending the day talking negotiation strategy.

"No need to negotiate; I'll take care of the check," I said, placing my credit card down on the tray.

Flabbergasted, my client said, "I thought one of your principles was holding your ground. You told us never to fold like that!"

"Let me finish. I will pick up dinner if you do something for me." I responded.

"Like what?"

"I'll cover the cost of our meal if you agree to send an email to the entire executive team recommending my services. And copy me on that email."

The executive glanced at the bill's total one more time and said, "I think we have a deal."

I paid the $800 restaurant tab, and he kept his promise. To date, that short negotiation netted me more than a quarter-million dollars in additional business. I schedule dinner with all clients and always expect them to "negotiate" the bill.

A small point that can add significant profit to your deals. For some reason, salespeople like to think in whole numbers. They concede in 5, 10, and even 15 percentage-point increments. If the customer wants a 5-percent reduction, can you get the same result with a 1.5-percent or 1.35-percent reduction? Never give the customer exactly the amount they are demanding. That sets a low bar and begs the other side to ask for more.

Once you determine the items in play, protect those that cost your company the most. Again, if you can get a sale at list price and a "free lunch," take the client to lunch. Salespeople mistake trying to get the customer to "bite" by offering larger concessions than are necessary. Price is the most quantifiable part of a negotiation and often the most expensive to give up. Many terms and conditions have a high cost as well. Post-sales support and service, generous payment terms, delivery charges, these things can erode the profitability of a deal even while maintaining your "price."

That is not to say you don't trade them for things you and your side might want or need but be careful. As a former sales manager, it was frustrating when my people gave away valuable add-ons to "sweeten" the deal even with added "sweetener" wasn't needed.

Sometimes, it pays to let the other side quantify the value of a concession for you instead of suggesting a value yourself. If you can get them to quantify the value, it sometimes gets you more than anticipated.

My older daughter, Alexis, was flying home from school a couple of winters ago; she was scheduled to arrive three days before Christmas. The airline, which I will not name, ran out of deicing fluid, and their flights were canceled for days. (I found this strange, as many of their flights are to Alaska.)

After much frustration dealing with the airline's customer service department, she was able to get a flight home arriving on Christmas Eve. And after her much-shortened holiday, I called the airline's customer service department to negotiate recompense.

As I explained the situation, the customer service agent pulled out the usual excuses, "No one could have predicted a storm lasting that long, sir."

"Actually, that isn't true. This storm was forecasted for at least a week. Your company could have planned better." I countered.

"Yes, but the snow affected all our flights. We had no way to get her home."

"You could have put her on another airline. They continued to operate service in and out of Seattle. The ticketing agent refused to do that." I obfuscated.

Finally, in a frustrated tone, she asked me, "What would you like me to do, Mr. Reilly?"

Now, I had her right where I wanted her, "I think you and your airline should figure that out. How much is my daughter missing two days with her family worth?"

"I don't know, Mr. Reilly. What would you have us do?"

(At this point, my daughter, who was listening to the exchange from her bedroom, shouted, "Ask them for a pony?")

In exasperation, the customer service agent said, "Would it be acceptable if we refunded the entire ticket?"

"That would make me happy. It will make me even happier if you throw in a couple of first-class upgrade coupons for the inconvenience." My response more of a statement than a question.

"I think we can do that."

And everyone was happy. No, scratch that — I was happy. Sometimes letting the other side confirm the value can be in your best interest.

When using this tactic, be prepared to play the waiting game. Even if at first the other side doesn't have a good response, give them time. They'll come up with something. You might be surprised. I was.

I have a good friend whose husband was considering a job with a competitor. His interview with the head of the company was the following day, and he knew a salary discussion would be an important part of the meeting. He asked me how much of an increase over his current salary was reasonable to ask for.

Instead, I suggested he ask his future boss, "How much do you think a guy with my skills and experience is worth?"

Worked like a charm.

The VP's offered him a starting salary 15 percent higher than he expected. Of course, I told him to request one extra week of vacation. He got that too.

Another favored trick of tough negotiators is getting you to negotiate with yourself. By refusing your original offer as unreasonable and telling you to revise and resubmit, they give nothing and get something. "These numbers are not going to work. Go back and sharpen your pencil and give us something realistic?" If you do as the buyer asks, you are negotiating against yourself and in the dark. Salespeople submit re-priced proposals all the time, which sets a terrible negotiation precedent.

Instead, insist the customer provide some guidance before revising your proposal. Something like, "Can you give me an idea of how far off they are?" or "I'm sorry, but you'll have to be more specific. I can't simply go back and redo my numbers without something to work with."

Be persistent. Tough negotiators become unresponsive to emails or voice mails, waiting you out hoping you give ground without any work on their end. Resist the urge to re-bid to get their attention.

TRADING CONCESSIONS TACTIC #4
Challenge their counteroffers.

You've heard the saying, "Once an offer is on the table, the next person who speaks loses." That's not true. Although silence can be an effective tactic in some negotiation situations, challenging a counteroffer is much more effective.

Resist the tendency of counteroffering without challenging the previous counter from the customer. Keep hardball buyers off-balance by questioning every counteroffer they make. Not many are used to having their counters challenged, making it more difficult for them to go on the offensive. Challenge counteroffers the same way you challenge the first offer, "How did you arrive at that counteroffer?" or "What makes that counter fair?"

Be persistent and irritating.

Let's go back to Greg and the FedEx story.

Greg says to me, "I can't give you the volume discount on this order, but we can offer you a 20-percent discount on your next order."

I would challenge that with something like, "Where did you get the 20 percent on the next order figure?"

Greg might respond, "What do you mean?"

"You're offering me a 20-percent discount on my next order. How about 10 percent on this order and 10 percent on the next? It is the same thing, really."

Just as you can challenge their counteroffer, expect them to challenge yours. Be prepared to respond to the same questions, "How did you arrive at that counter?" and "What makes that fair?" And so on.

Have a good defense prepared for your counteroffers with a logical argument and strong value proposition.

From here, the process becomes iterative: counteroffer-challenge-counteroffer-challenge, and so forth. Both sides grind away at each other until one side runs out of room to maneuver. At that point, the negotiation moves into its end-stage—time for a Best and Final Offer.

The Rocky Story

BUYING TIME

I had to buy some time and needed to de-value the Wheaten ... make Rocky into a commodity as best I could. Challenging the $1,200 as a "good price" was my initial strategy.

I considered some potential tactics. I could make an offer and tell the store owner to take it or leave it. I could find a cheaper dog at the shop, pretend to be interested and use the lower price to get a discount. I could bluff and tell him I was prepared to drive to Spokane despite the risks.

In realty though, to keep my promise, I knew there were no other options.

But that didn't leave me completely without a negotiation strategy. Anticipating that I would most likely need to give ground, I considered what to ask for in return. The pet store had a secondary business of boarding dogs for extended periods of time. As my business often takes me out of town at the last minute, I might throw some kennel nights into the mix. They wouldn't cost Ralph much, a handful of dog food, a bowl of water. Living in a dog-pampered city like Seattle, those services can get quite expensive. Perhaps I could get some things for the dog; a bed, leash, or something else I might need as a new dog owner. It was worth a shot if Ralph wouldn't budge.

As long as Ralph didn't know my situation, I still had leverage. As long as he didn't know that this dog already had a name.

I needed time.

"Hi, Ralph. This is Steve again."

"Steve?" Oh, for Christ's sake!

"Yeah, Steve. The guy interested in the Wheaten."

"Right. Did you want to make a deal on this dog?"

"I don't have time right now. I'm headed out of town and wanted to ask you to hold the dog until I get back?"

"I don't usually do that without some earnest money, some money down to hold the dog."

He wanted "skin in the game."

"What's your policy on deposits?"

"I require at least 25% to hold a dog."

"I'm guessing it's non-refundable."

'That's our policy, but if you decide you don't want the Wheaten, you can use that money for another dog or supplies, food, grooming stuff, whatever."

"I'd rather not since we haven't fully decided on a dog just yet. Unless, of course, you're willing to cut the price right now and do a deal over the phone."

Maybe he'd bite.

"Steve, like I said, this dog is worth the money because..."

I cut him off.

"I know, I know, Ralph. I heard you earlier. Well, at least give me right-of-first-refusal for 24 hours."

"What do you mean?"

"I mean that if someone comes in and wants to buy the Wheaten, you call and give me the option to buy him first."

"But what if they're willing to pay full price? "

"Let's cross that bridge if and when we come to it."

"Hmm, okay. But remember, if I get a full price offer, I am going to sell the dog."

"But you call me first, right?"

"Okay, but only until the end of the day tomorrow. Once we close for the day, I can sell the dog to whomever I want."

Chapter 3

Best and Final Offers Strategy and Tactics

"Is that your final offer?" the chief sourcing officer asked.

My client, an aerospace company, was close to a deal with an offshore manufacturer of an important airframe component. After some initial grandstanding and positioning, both sides settled into a six-month comfortable but wary negotiating environment that included three counteroffers each and multiple meetings. Most line items were agreed upon, but there were still outstanding delivery issues, post-sale service, and support. Despite that, the manufacturer did not understand what he was asking for at this particular point in the negotiation.

I wanted to be sure.

"Are you asking for our best and final offer?"

"Yes, I am asking if this is the best you can do."

"Perhaps you don't realize what you are asking."

"I think I do. I'm asking whether or not this is your best and final offer. Seems pretty clear to me."

"Yes, but a best and final offer is a serious request. Don't you think?"

"Not really. You give us your best shot, and we will then give you our best shot," he answered testily.

"That's not a best and final," I said.

"What do you mean?"

"If we present our best and final offer, you have to decide to take it or leave it."

"No, no. That's not a best and final offer. A best and final offer is your last, best price. Then we counter that and see if we can reach an agreement."

"That's not the way we work. When we give our best and final offer, you can choose to take it or leave it. That is why it's called a 'best and final offer,'" I said.

Frustrated, he stepped back. "Maybe we aren't ready for your best and final at this point. So, this is just a counteroffer on the table, right?"

"Yes. But if you'd like us to take this back and rework it as a best and final offer, we can do that."

"No, no. I don't think we've reached that point."

"I agree."

Best and Final Offer Strategy

One of the trickiest parts of negotiating is holding the ground you've spent time and effort protecting while trying to bring a deal to a close. Depending on how well you've defended your price, you may or may not have a good deal at this point, but even if you've held your ground and carved out a good deal, tough customers will "nibble" at it until you end up with a less-profitable agreement than you thought.

There is an almost universal misconception about Best and Final Offers. In many industries proposing multiple Best and Final Offers is the norm. When negotiators accept counters after the final offer, it quickly becomes acceptable and when done enough times, it becomes standard procedure. And even though one side may use the term, they do not consider it the end of the negotiation.

But in other industries, a Best and Final Offer is always best and always final. The party making the final offer asks the other side to accept or reject it with no counteroffer. When used as it should, making a Best and Final Offer is intended to bring the counteroffering process to a close. That is how it is supposed to work in theory.

Reality, however, is more complex.

Good negotiators wear you down; it's part of their strategy. A negotiation can be a long process. You have to resist the urge to give in due to impatience, irritation, or exhaustion. That said, the counteroffering process can't go on forever; at some point, one side or the other runs out of room to maneuver. Then it is time to bring the negotiation to a close. It is a tricky and sometimes fatal phase if poorly navigated.

Negotiators can tire of back-and-forth at times and make unnecessary concessions to "get a deal done." This is a mistake.

Patience is critical in large, complex negotiations. Hospital/Insurer negotiations take more than six months with dozens of counteroffers. This may seem like a long time until you consider that an extensive hospital system can have more than $300 million in reimbursement at risk, and the same for an insurer. A deliberate and cautious strategy is in both sides' best interest.

In negotiation, the quicker you reach a deal, the more likely one side left more money on the table than necessary. If you make the first offer, and the other side takes it immediately, you most likely misread your degree of leverage. You probably could have asked for more or offered less. The reverse is true, as well. If the other side makes an unexpectedly attractive offer, be cautious before accepting it. There may be some hidden costs you have not anticipated.

Bottom Line

One of the most important pieces of a negotiation strategy is the concept of a "bottom line." A bottom line is the worst deal you will accept. Agreeing to a deal that is the same as your bottom line is not success. It isn't a good deal, but at least you have a deal. Some negotiators are relieved when they get a deal close to but above their bottom line. This is wrong thinking. The best measure of your negotiation's success is the gap between your First Offer and the final deal.

Identifying your bottom line before entering negotiations is another key step to success. Let's return to the used car example. If you remember the scenario, we decided to list the car for $17,000. But before listing it, we decide that any offer lower than $12,500 is unacceptable. In other words, if we get offers at $12,499 or less, we will reject them. This makes $12,500 our bottom line. Based on the response or lack of response to our ad, we may need to rethink our bottom line.

Knowing your bottom line can keep you from being taken advantage of or agreeing to a deal that doesn't "make sense."

That said, companies agree all the time to deals that don't seem to make sense. Usually, this means the deal doesn't make sense from a dollar and cents perspective, but for some other reason. Some companies will lose money on a deal to gain market share, while others will make an unprofitable deal to get a "name" customer to improve their brand. A salesperson may not think the deal makes sense, but senior management might.

A flexible bottom line is better than one that is rigid. An inflexible bottom line can blow up a negotiation even when there is a good chance to reach agreement. Using the phrase "I would never . . .!" sabotages negotiations and keep a party from reaching an agreement that might be in their best interest. Best to view a bottom line as a guideline, not a rule. And sometimes you have no choice but to take a deal well below your bottom line.

During the economic collapse of the housing market in 2008 – 2009, sellers found themselves in the difficult position of trying to get out of a mortgage that was worth more than their house. Homeowners found themselves with little to no leverage as the value of their homes collapsed. For those who were able to sell their homes, many had to sell well below their bottom line.

In every hospital-insurer negotiation, both sides have an idea of the "worst deal they will accept." But as discussions progress, one or both sides often revise that number due to added information or changing market conditions. If a medical insurer decides it will not raise hospital reimbursement rates more than eight (8) percent regardless of the situation, their opening offer might a five percent increase, giving them room to maneuver. It's a good intention, but as the offer and counteroffers fly, insurers often realize (just as in the used car negotiation) that 8 percent was unrealistic and that going higher with important reciprocal concessions is actually a good deal.

Some bottom lines seem so fundamental that common sense tells you never to cross that line; like paying full sticker price for a new automobile. But even that can be a mistake.

Recently, I was in the market for a new car and made the rounds to the local dealers. After negotiating several significant discounts, I visited one last dealer before making a final decision. With multiple excellent deals to choose from, there was minimal risk sharing the details of the other dealer's discounts with the salesperson. If the dealership could beat these deals, I would consider it. If not, I'd buy my new car from the one with the best deal.

The salesperson's first question threw me.

"Do you know the typically yearly return rate of your retirement funds and other investments?"

Being in business for myself, I pay attention to my investment returns.

"I do pretty well. My return rate was a little more than 12 percent last year."

The salesperson paused, then asked, "All the deals with the other car dealers have one thing in common; the bigger your down payment, the deeper the discount."

"Yes, that's right. Skin in the game gave me more leverage."

"Do you keep all that cash on hand?"

"I have some liquid investments to draw from." I added, very sure of myself, "Don't worry. I have the money."

He politely pounced.

"I'm sure you do but tying up all that money in a depreciating asset doesn't make sense."

"I don't see what you are getting at," put off by his cocksure attitude.

"If you kept the down payment money where it is, even at a conservative five-percent return, that would be better than putting it into an asset that loses value every day."

"Don't worry, I have the money."

"I'm sure you do. But what if you could keep your money where it is and still have the car you want."

"How do I do that?"

"If you were able to get the car you want without a down payment and no-interest loan, would you be interested?"

"What's the catch?" I'd been at this too long to assume there wasn't one.

"The only catch is that to get this offer, you have to pay full price."

"You mean sticker price?"

"Yes, it is the only way we can make money on this type of deal. It is a one-time offer to move last year's models off the lot."

As it happened, the dealership was having a special financing offer of zero down payment with zero percent financing. This end-of-the-year special was designed to deplete the dealer's inventory before the new year models and styles arrived. The one non-negotiable point was that the deal was only available to a buyer who paid the full sticker price.

Not fully understanding the financial complexity behind this offer, I called my accountant. I couldn't figure out whether this deal was better than the negotiated discounts with the other dealers. I needed some guidance regarding the financial/tax incentives laid out in the dealer's proposal. I explained the offer of zero down with zero percent interest.

"Is this the car you want?" he asked.

"Yes, I've narrowed my search down to this make and model."

He said without hesitation, "Take the deal."

"Are you sure?" I asked.

"Absolutely. It is the best deal. Take it."

"Really? Even though I have to pay the full sticker price!"

"It's the best deal by far."

In 20 years, he never steered me wrong, so I took the deal.

Later, he explained the time value of money in this situation. He said that the car's price fell for every month that passed, and the longer the payment plan, the less the car cost. Assuming a two percent inflation rate and zero interest, the car cost me less every year; the longer I took to pay the car off, the less it cost me.

At the beginning of my car shopping expedition, if someone had told me I would pay the full asking price, I would have thought they were nuts. But new information and a few quick calculations made it obvious that I needed to change – even disregard -my original bottom line.

Never say never, as they say.

WALK-AWAY OPTION (PLAN B)

There are times when it no longer makes sense to continue negotiations. Sometimes, the best plan of action is to walk away. Walking away is terminating the negotiation altogether; it is breaking off discussions and moving on: no more counteroffers, no more haggling, no more deal. You accept that you will never agree on this particular negotiation with this specific person or entity; you decide your Plan B is better than your Plan A.

Using the car scenario, if you are serious about holding the line and don't receive any offers above $12,499, hopefully, you have a Plan B and/or C, D, etc. In this situation, there are multiple possible walk away options. Plan B might be to donate the car to charity; Plan C is to use it as a trade-in, Plan D is to continue to drive it.

When selling a house, if you receive offers below your bottom line or no offers at all, your Plan B might be to convert the home into a rental unit or remodel it and place it back on the market when conditions improve. You could decide to live in it until the market turns more in your favor, or you could walk away from the mortgage. (I am not suggesting you do that. Just pointing it out as an option.)

This brings us to the concept of BATNA.

Readers familiar with *Getting to Yes* may remember this term. The Best Alternative to a Negotiated Agreement or BATNA is a relatively simple idea of using your walk-away option. BATNA is your Plan B; what you will do if you can't reach an agreement. It is your alternative to continuing to bargain and attempting to get a deal.

Ury and Fisher posit that anyone can walk away from any negotiation, and by identifying your walk-away option, you can have more negotiation confidence. They advocate walking away from more powerful opponents to avoid giving away the store, or at the very least, taking a deal that doesn't "make sense." The authors purport that you protect yourself from difficult opponents by having a good BATNA.

In theory, this may be true, but in the world of selling, it is folly.

For those of us who spent a significant portion of our careers in sales, we would never just up and walk away from a potential deal, no matter how slim the chances. That goes against our nature as a salesperson and disregards one of the most important attitudes contributing to our success: irrational optimism in the face of inevitable defeat.

Telling a salesperson to walk away from a possible deal is a bit cavalier for someone who never had to achieve a quota to hold onto a job. Technically, you might have the ability to abort negotiations on a big deal, but you still have a sales goal to make. That said, salespeople are always better negotiators when they've already reached their quota because they don't need the business. Salespeople are much better at holding their ground when they don't feel desperate.

From time to time, I meet a person who previously attended the Getting to Yes seminar, and when I do, I always ask, "What do you remember most about the Ury and Fisher approach?" The universal answer is, "To make sure I know my BATNA."

Though most can't recall what the initials stand for, they believe that knowing your options empowers them a bit. It's a bit curious that the term most remembered from a course designed specifically to improve negotiation skills is one that describes how to walk away from the table — in other words, refusing to continue the negotiation.

Keep in mind that your customer on the other side of the table also has walk-away options. The difference between their walk-away and your walk-away is called leverage.

Leverage

Leverage is the ability to influence the decisions and actions of your opponent. A negotiator uses leverage to get a better deal or coerce the other side to concede. It is an integral part of any negotiation. In situations in which you have good walk-away options, you usually have the upper hand. In cases in which your walk-away choice sucks, the other side has the upper hand. The more leverage you have, the more likely you will reach an agreement that meets your goals in a negotiation.

There are three different possibilities to consider regarding leverage.

When You Need Them, More Than They Need You

In this situation, the other side has a better walk away option than you. They can use this leverage to get a better deal putting you at a disadvantage if you aren't familiar with techniques for eroding their power.

Consider the current Seattle housing market. House prices are climbing faster than almost anywhere in the US for a couple of reasons. First, the local economy is on fire. Add to that the limited space for housing in central Seattle as it sits sandwiched between Puget Sound on the west and Lake Washington on the east. Lastly, the Emerald City is a Who's Who of Corporate Industry with Amazon, Starbucks, Microsoft, Boeing, and many others calling it home.

It is a seller's market with houses selling at their listing price or higher. It's a seller's market because the buyer needs the seller more than the opposite.

When They Need You More Than You Need Them

In this situation, your walk-away option(s) are better than theirs. You have the upper hand, and it should translate into better deals because you are in the driver's seat; you have more leverage.

Try to determine who needs who more in this situation:

When I am in the market for a new iPhone or MacBook, Craigslist is the first place I look. For those of you who immediately dismiss me as crazy, let me explain. Although the latest release phone or computer is often not available, or at least not available at a significant discount, there is always a plethora of later-model phones and computers to choose from. I search for sellers in my hometown (I only do face-to-face transactions) and look for a latest- model gadget in good condition with all the software and updates. It saves me money, as Applications can add hundreds of dollars to a store-bought computer and phone.

Once I find the item I want, I arrange to meet the seller at a local coffee shop (not hard to find in Seattle.). Meeting in a safe, well-lit, and crowded venue eliminates the chance of being scammed or robbed. When the seller and I connect, I have them run the device through its paces to ensure everything works. Once I determine the machine is in good working order, I have the seller wipe the hard drive clean of all their files, except software.

Who has the better walk-away option at this point in the transaction, the seller or me?

If for some reason, the seller and I can't reach an agreement, I don't even have to leave the coffee shop to find another computer or phone using the Craigslist App. The seller has to wait for another potential buyer to contact them and arrange a sale.

That gives me more leverage. The seller has taken the time to meet with me, run the device through its paces, and maybe even paid for my cup of coffee; that is all skin in the game. Whether I use this leverage or not to get a better price is another matter. But even if I choose not to, I am in a stronger negotiating position. Of course, the seller can take his BATNA and walk away, but the time and energy invested make it less likely that will happen.

I have a client who makes the world's most accurate and shortest time-to-result infectious disease tests on the market. It saves time, money, effort, and, most importantly, lives. They have an exclusive market position with heavy demand from hospitals and physicians. Still, the company salespeople heavily discount and almost always give away a not-insignificant amount of "free" product.

Why? Not because their customers play hardball; they often don't. All they do is ask nicely, and the salespeople accommodate them. I am not saying discounting is always wrong, but when salespeople discount and receive nothing in return, they could do a better job. Giving ground when in a strong position is poor negotiating.

When Neither Can Live Without The Other

Sometimes called the "nuclear option," in this situation, neither side can afford to walk away; the damage would be too great. The shared pain of a failed negotiation is too much for either side. Playing hardball is not in either side's best interest. Better to work through to an acceptable or mutually disagreeable agreement to avoid assured mutual destruction.

It is common for aircraft manufacturers to use a sole-source supplier for a critical part like an aircraft wing or fuselage. A company like Boeing is equally reliant on suppliers' performance, as the supplier is on Boeing. In this case, win-win strategies work best; when both sides realize this interdependency and work toward collaborative solutions. That doesn't mean giving away the store; it means that searching for shared interests and mutually beneficial outcomes should be a priority. Playing hardball does long-term damage, especially in matters of trust.

Fake Leverage is Leverage

A couple of years ago, a major health insurer and the largest hospital chain in Seattle tried to negotiate an end-of-year agreement. My insurer client asked for my help when the hospital chain began making unreasonable demands. The dealbreaker came when the hospital administrator demanded reimbursement increases unsustainable. The requested increases were so large that the insurer would not be competitive in the Seattle market if it met the hospital's demands; it would lose money for years.

Again and again, the hospital system administrator threatened to go "non-par" or non-participating. If that were allowed to happen, all the hospitals and clinics would become "out-of-network" for thousands of employees in the greater Northwest. Every health plan member would need to find new doctors and new hospitals or pay hefty out-of-network bills. Looking to win the battle in public, the hospital hired a PR firm to place articles in local newspapers describing the health plan as a "bad faith negotiator."

In frustration and desperation, the insurer called the administrator's bluff by making a genuine Best and Final Offer which was immediately rejected. In the final meeting between the two parties, my client told the hospital to begin communicating the network's anticipated disruption to their patients via a "termination letter." (This is a legal requirement in most states if a hospital and insurer cannot reach an agreement.) The administrator stormed out of the meeting, threatening to sue the insurer and "put them out of business" in the state of Washington.

After a week of uncomfortable radio silence, the other shoe dropped.

Chastised and chagrined, the hospital administrator asked for a secret meeting to accept the insurer's Best and Final Offer. The insurer agreed but with one additional concession. The hospital's public relations firm had to retract the earlier article stating the insurer was a trustworthy business partner focused on its members' health and welfare.

If my client hadn't called the administrators bluff, even though the hospital had no intention of following through on the threat, that gambit would have been successful. When perceived leverage works, then it is leverage. When it doesn't, then it is an idle threat.

Bluffing becomes riskier the more that is at risk, the higher the stakes, the riskier the bluff. When a bluff works, then it gives you an advantage. When it doesn't, it leaves you weakened in this and future negotiations. As was the case in this situation, it left the hospital in a weak position for future negotiations. Idle threats lose their power, the more they are used.

I run into situations where it is obvious a customer is bluffing, but the salesperson still caves. A semi-conductor client needed help slowing the rate their profit margin was eroding. This seemed strange to me considering this particular industry's market dynamics.

The entire market for dynamic random-access memory, or DRAM, was in the midst of a severe shortage of available product due to manufacturing constraints. Computer manufacturers were "allocated" a specific amount of DRAM chips per month by the manufacturers. Their allocated amount was always less than they wanted and constrained their ability to produce enough computers to meet demand. Every manufacturer and supplier was in the same position.

Despite this constrained market, my client was experiencing significant erosion of its Average Selling Price (ASP). It turned out that the computer manufacturer buyers were threatening to shift the business to other suppliers if they didn't get additional discounts. Their salespeople felt the need to provide price breaks as acts of goodwill.

However, in spite of making threats to switch the business, other manufacturers had no available product to sell. The buyers were using a salesperson's natural fear of losing the business to get even deeper discounts. The only thing they got in return for the additional discount was to keep the business they would have kept anyway.

No Leverage but a Good Deal

Experts say that the person with the most power in a negotiation is the one who can walk away: the customer with many alternative products, the buyer with multiple approved vendors, the purchasing agent who doesn't have an urgent need for a product or service. This is not always the case.

The car dealer/customer power dynamic illustrates how it is possible to reach a favorable outcome despite being in a weaker negotiating position. Who has the power in a car negotiation? The customer, of course. Any customer can walk out of the dealership whenever they want; dealers have to wait for another to walk in. Yet, even though potential car buyers have more alternatives, car dealers cut deals that favor their interests.

How is it that dealers sell cars with high-profit margins with such weak leverage? By keeping customers in the game. They neutralize the customers' willingness to walk away. The time you put into negotiation is called "skin in the game." The more skin in the game, the less likely you are to walk. They know this and use it to their advantage. Studies by car dealer associations show that the strongest predictor of whether you buy a car in a specific dealership on any given day is the length of time you spend in the dealership that day: the hours wasted haggling. Dealers know that the more time you spend "haggling," the less likely you will find another dealership and subject yourself to the same process.

To you, those hours seem wasted, but they are invaluable to car dealers.

I'm not suggesting you confine your customers in a small office with bad coffee until they buy. Probably not the best way to win them over. But tough negotiators are patient and wear you down by keeping you in the game. The best salespeople are good at keeping customers engaged while holding their ground.

Best and Final Offer Tactics

BEST AND FINAL TACTIC #1
Identify the other side's walk-away options.

Knowing your BATNA can keep you from being taken advantage of but evaluating the strength of your opponent's walk-away options prevents caving to idle threats. Before capitulating to customer Best and Final Offers, ask yourself how serious the customer is about giving the business to your competition.

The "Big Machine" market is very competitive. Caterpillar has the most market share with also-rans John Deere and Komatsu positioning themselves as the lower-cost alternatives to win business. Price is an important factor in deciding which machine to buy, but after-sale service, support, and replacement parts can be just as important. Many large construction companies use Caterpillar machines exclusively; they refer to them as "CAT shops." A CAT Shop uses Caterpillar machines almost exclusively and, in return, gets aggressive pricing on replacement parts, service and support, and co-marketing dollars.

CAT Shops following through on a threat to convert to a "Komatsu shop" is highly unlikely as it entails very high tangible and intangible costs. Despite this, many buyers attempt to use this idle threat as leverage to get a better price. And while CAT is sensitive to their customer's cost pressures, an idle threat doesn't improve the working relationship.

So, before conceding, evaluate the switching costs the customer would incur by changing from your product to your competitor. The higher the switching costs, the more likely buyers are making a threat they can't follow through with. Like with the CAT shops, being the incumbent gives you a distinct negotiation advantage. Good negotiators will pretend they're willing to absorb the switching costs even when they have no intention of making such a drastic change. "We'll just give the business to your competitor'" may be a bluff, maybe not. The trick is recognizing an idle threat when you hear one.

Sometimes you can educate the other side that the costs

of walking away outweigh the benefits. Often, switching costs don't occur to many people until they are in the middle of paying them. If you can convince them that negotiating is a better option, sometimes they will engage.

Elliott Bay Books is one of Seattle's finest bookstores. It has a great selection, helpful staff, an atmosphere conducive to browsing, and, of course, a Seattle-class coffee shop. A couple of years ago, I was casually browsing the shelves when I happened upon a book of prints by a famous French impressionist. I instantly thought of an artist friend whose birthday was that coming weekend and the book would make a much-appreciated gift.

I happened to notice that the back cover had a small, delaminated section. Barely noticeable, but for a $70 coffee table book, it was unacceptable, unless... I asked a clerk if there was another copy. There wasn't. He said the store could have a new book within a month if I were willing to wait.

That wouldn't work for me, so I decided to negotiate.

"I wanted it as a gift for a friend. Any chance you can get me a copy by Saturday?"

"No, sorry, but we will call you as soon as it comes in."

"If I were to buy this book with this delamination, can you discount it?"

The clerk pulled the book off the counter and placed it on the shelf behind the register, and snipped, "Sorry, sir. We don't negotiate."

Like a bass to bait, I rose to the occasion. "Do you mind if I speak with the store manager?"

"He'll tell you the same thing. We don't negotiate prices on books. It is what it is."

Not necessarily, I thought.

"You've been helpful, but I'd still like to clarify the store policy on damaged books with the manager."

The clerk went away with a snort, and a young man, the store manager I supposed, came and took her place. I showed him the delaminated book and explained that it wasn't worth the cover price in its present condition though I wanted to buy it.

"I understand, sir, but we don't negotiate books. We return them to the distributor for full credit."

I had anticipated his response. "Let me understand something. By full credit, you mean full credit for the cost of the book, not for the retail price of the book."

"Yes, that's right."

"I understand that. But I am surprised you are willing to wait a month for a book to be restocked and then wait for some interested party to come in and buy it. If that happens at all."

"That's our policy."

"I understand. But I am offering to take a damaged book off your hands for a reasonable profit. Your policy doesn't make sense to me as a businessman."

He paused, took a step back, and asked, "Well, how much would you pay for the book, then?"

I smiled and replied, "How much of a discount do you think a book with a delaminated cover is reasonable?"

And so, it goes.

Recently a salesperson complained to me that his manager sabotaged his negotiation strategy by telling him just before a customer meeting, "We have to get this deal, or we won't make our end-of-year numbers. We can't afford to let this one get away."

"When my manager says that, he doesn't realize that the thought and strategy I put into my plan is out the window."

I asked why.

"If I don't get this sale, my boss is going to kill me."

I asked, "Does the customer know that your boos will kill you if you don't get this sale?"

"Well, no."

"Then why would you change your strategy?"

"Because I know I can't walk away. And that's what matters."

Not necessarily.

The only time you should alter your negotiation strategy is if the other side knows you are desperate. Good negotiators hold their cards as close to the vest as the other side dictates. If the other side doesn't know that you have no Plan B, don't tell them. And even if the other side confronts you about your limited walk away, a good negotiator will bluff and pretend there are many options and alternatives. Even if customers think you are in a poor negotiation position, with a bit of bravado and bluffing, you may convince them that you are in a better position than they think.

I work with a start-up company that has innovative and groundbreaking technology but a small client base. Every deal and every dollar are crucial to the company. The most common challenge they hear from potential customers is: "This product is new and untested. We might be able to do a deal, but we are going to need a significant discount to take a chance like this."

With a bit of bravado and confidence, they respond with, "Our company has deliberately targeted you and your company as early adopters. We decided on a select customer base for marketing purposes. The deal we are offering is our introductory price. Once we have a significant market share, which we will, this introductory price will no longer be available."

Now it's their move.

Best and Final Tactic #2
Be the first to ask for their Best and Final Offer.

No one can tell you how many counteroffers should be on the table before you ask the other side for their Best and Final Offer. In some industries, multiple counteroffers are standard operating procedure, whereas, in others, it can be offer, counteroffer, deal.

But at some point, it becomes apparent one side or the other is running out of room to maneuver – that one side is approaching their bottom line. Figuring out when your opponent is nearing this point takes skill; a negotiator must feel the opponent's tension, look for signs of stiffening positions, and intuit when the other side is nearing their limit. But there are things negotiators do that indicate when it's time to put them on the spot and ask for their Best and Final Offer.

When good negotiators give ground, they do so in diminishing increments, smaller and smaller concessions. Pay attention to the value of each concession as you haggle through the process. The first concession you get from a car dealer is likely the biggest – not necessarily the last, but the biggest. Expect the dealership to give less and less ground with every counter. Shrinking counteroffers is a sign they are reaching their limit.

Another indicator is the length of time between each counteroffer. Typically, the longer they wait, the closer they are to their bottom line. Car dealers keep you waiting longer and longer periods between each counteroffer to see if you will throw in the towel and sign on the dotted line; it's part of the game. But two can play that game. If you hang in there long enough, they will often make additional, albeit smaller, concessions.

Tough negotiators want to keep you in the game as long as they can to wring out last-minute concessions. A car dealer will let you walk to your car before calling to tell you to come back in and talk about it. Return the favor. Using all your skills and reading their body language, push the other side as far as you think you can. Then ask for their Best and Final Offer.

BEST AND FINAL TACTIC #3
Never let anyone counter your Best and Final Offer.

When you decide to make a proper Best and Final Offer, never make another concession. A Best and Final Offer means you are willing to lose the deal if the other side turns it down. To cough up another concession is to weaken your position in this and future negotiations. The only acceptable response to a Best and Final is a "thumbs up" or "thumbs down." If you have decided to stand your ground, then accept the consequences.

One of the most frequent challenges I encountered as an instructor of the *Getting to Yes* workshop was how to respond to the question, "Is that your Best and Final Offer?" Our scripted response was, "In win-win negotiation, neither side ever has to make a Best and Final Offer because you always come to a mutually beneficial agreement." Again, good in theory, but there are many situations in which that won't work. In binding arbitration and labor negotiations, for example, Best and Final Offers are often legally mandated.

How do you respond to the question, "Is this your Best and Final Offer?"

"Yes" is the wrong answer if you're unwilling to lose the deal. No" is another wrong response if you still have room left to maneuver and want to protect it. Telling a tough negotiator your last offer isn't your Best and Final opens the door to losing additional ground. I searched for a response that would be tough and flexible to protect a negotiator from pressure but leave the door open to possible options. If I hadn't ended up dealing with hospital negotiations, I would have never figured it out.

The best response is, "We feel that this is a good deal and the best we can do. But if you have something additional to discuss, throw it on the table; we will consider it." Or another version: "This is the best we can do, but I am willing to negotiate further if you have something you'd like to discuss."

Both these responses take the pressure off the negotiator to give more ground and puts it back on the other side to make the next move. It ensures you don't give more ground without a reciprocal concession, even if you still have ground to give.

If you are making a genuine true Best and Final Offer, these responses leave the door open for something you've may have overlooked or for an additional concession from the other side that might be in your best interest.

I have been surprised by the number of useful responses generated by these questions. On several occasions, they opened up entire negotiation areas my clients never considered.

Even after a Best and Final Offer is on the table, it might be in your best interest to continue to negotiate if the other side offers something of value. But if they don't, and if you are genuinely making your Best and Final Offer, the only option for the other side is to take the deal or walk.

Best and Final Tactic #4
Always counter their Best and Final Offer.

Never let the other side counter your final offer but always counter theirs. Once you've coaxed out their Best and Final Offer, counter it; always ask for one more thing. Even if their Best and Final Offer meets your criteria of a good deal, ask for more, especially with a tough customer. This last concession tests the other side's limit and keeps them on the defensive. If they've presented their Best and Final and then they give more ground, counter that as well.

Using this "just one more little thing" technique runs counter to a win-win philosophy. It is counter-collaborative and characterized by some as playing dirty; it's a legitimate charge from win-win proponents. But it's fair game against difficult negotiators, and if you don't, expect that they will. Tough negotiators don't stop asking for things until they've squeezed out as much as possible in a deal. Getting comfortable with this tactic against any negotiator can incrementally improve deal after deal. But be reasonable and avoid asking for something that could be a dealbreaker.

Best to stick with a "bag of dog food." (You will understand "bag of dog food" after reading the rest of the Rocky Story.)

I worked with the CIO of a major networking company negotiating with a critical supplier. After two weeks of back-and-forth of hard bargaining and multiple counteroffers, his "little thing" was a demand that the supplier guarantee safety stock for a critical replacement part into perpetuity. His inflexibility and unreasonable demand sabotaged the deal and damaged the relationship for years.

Follow these rules when considering a Best and Final Offer from a zero-sum negotiator.

First, determine if the offer is acceptable as it currently stands. Ask yourself if you can live with the terms and conditions on the table without additional concessions. If you decide to take the deal, then take the offer but with … just one more little thing. It could sound like this, "We are happy to accept your offer and look forward to working with you on this. Just one little thing we'd like to request, and we can close this deal." You agree to their Best and Final Offer with a minor addition.

But because you found their Final Offer acceptable, if the customer balks at "one more little thing," pull the additional item off the table and take the original Best and Final Offer. Don't jeopardize an acceptable deal for one "little thing."

If you decide their Best and Final Offer is unacceptable, make a full counteroffer with further concessions from their side. Treat it as just another counteroffer. You have nothing to lose since you already decided to walk away, and it might keep them in the game. Who knows, you might be able to hammer out a better agreement if you just keep haggling. If not, you always have the option to walk away.

The day I went to pick up my new car, I met the finance officer in his office to finalize the title transfer signatures. He handed me a very nice Mont Blanc pen with the automobile manufacturer's logo to sign the proper documents.

I signed them all except the final and most important one, the deed transfer from the dealership. Looking up, I asked, "Does the company give you these pens, or do you pay for them yourselves?"

Looking a bit perplexed, the finance officer said, "Uh, the company gives them to us."

"So, they are free to you, right?"

"Yes, that's right."

Then with a dawning realization, he asked, "You'd like one of these pens, don't you?"

"I'd like two of these pens," I said.

"And you aren't going to sign that page unless I give you them, right?"

"I wouldn't say that the pen is a dealbreaker. But it could motivate me to write a good review on Yelp for your dealership."

Glancing sideways to the salesperson, he said, "I think we can do that."

Asking for one more little thing doesn't hurt. They can always say no, and you might be surprised by how many say yes.

This brings us to the endpoint of my negotiation process and this book's objective of reconciling win-win with zero-sum. Being collaborative is the central tenet of the win-win negotiation strategy. Being competitive is the central tenet of zero-sum or hardball. Trying to collaborate with someone who plays the "I win only if you lose" game will cost you. On the other hand, playing hardball when the other side is open to a more cooperative approach will damage your long-term interests.

I've tried to strike a realistic and effective balance between the conflicting approaches; to provide both strategy and tactics for protecting your interests against hardball and cooperative negotiators, emphasizing the tough approach. That doesn't mean you never share your interests with the other side. And it doesn't mean you always avoid win-win approaches. It does mean that until you have a foundation of trust and a "good read" of the other side's intentions, be careful, protect your interests.

If you indulge me, though, let me share some life wisdom that lends itself to negotiation.

For me, negotiation is a metaphor for life. If you would rather walk away from a difficult situation than hang in there and try to work it out, then you are out of the game more than in the game. If you always capitulate, if you would rather get a deal done than negotiate something better for your side, then you are also not in the game. Life is in the back-and-forth.

As I teach my daughters, a person can be tough and sensitive, trusting and cautious, thrifty and generous, brave, and humble. It doesn't always have to be a choice between one or the other. You have to develop the ability to read the other side and play along those continuums. Similarly, you can't take the same approach in every negotiation. Your negotiation stance must vary with each person, situation, and desired outcome.

With this book, you now have many more tools to evaluate the situation in front of you and negotiate accordingly. I wish you the best of luck in holding your ground.

The Rocky Story

"WTF?"

I'd bought myself a little time but needed a game plan. Ralph seemed set on the price and did a textbook job defending it. I was in a terrible negotiating position with no Plan B or at least none that wouldn't entail severe intangible costs.

I sat Maddy down to talk.

"Do you REALLY want this dog, honey? We can keep looking and maybe find a nicer, even better one."

"Nope. I feel like Rocky is my dog already, Dad. You never go back on your promises."

She added with a sulky tone, "But if we can't afford Rocky, I guess we can find a cheaper dog somewhere else."

"No, no, honey. You're right. We will get Rocky. I promise."

I flew to Houston the next day; that wasn't positioning. I was in the air all afternoon. When I landed, I half hoped to find a voicemail from Ralph offering a lower price. No such luck. I waited until the last minute to see if Ralph called me before I called him. I figured that if he called first, it might improve my leverage. Again, no such luck.

At 7:45 pm Houston time, the store was closing. It was now or never.

"Ralph here."

"This is Steve."

"Steve, who?" This is ridiculous.

"The guy interested in the Wheaten, the Wheaten Terrier."

"Oh yeah, right. You mean Rocky."

Long pause, deep breath. "Excuse me?"

"Steve, right? You and your daughter are getting the Wheaten, Rocky?"

WTF?

I played dumb. "I don't understand; who is Rocky?"

"Your dog. Your daughter named him Rocky, right?"

I played dumber, "I don't know what you're talking about. We are thinking about the dog but haven't made a decision yet."

"Your daughter and her mother were in my store today; she said you promised to get Rocky for her."

A dog with a name is a dog with a home.

"We bathed him and fixed him up with a collar, leash, and tags with his name and both phone numbers. He's ready to go. All I need is a check or credit card, and Rocky can go home with her today."

My strategy shattered; my leverage gone... I threw myself at Ralph's mercy.

"Ralph, you know, and I know that you have me over a barrel now."

"You think so?"

"Let me tell you what I do for a living."

"Okay..." Ralph was confused by my abrupt change in tone from master negotiator to fumbling doofus.

"I teach people how to negotiate."

"Really? Is that a good business? I should take one of those courses." He could teach my course.

"Why are you telling me this?" He asked.

"It's just that I was hoping to get a better deal for the dog.

It's tough for a person who makes his living negotiating to pay full price for anything, even a dog... Rocky."

"$1,200 is a good price for this dog. And you don't want to drive to Spokane if you don't have to."

"I know, Ralph, I know. Can you cut me a break? Can you do a little something for me on the price?"

Now Ralph changed his tone. "Steve, I want my dogs to go to good homes, and your daughter seems to love this dog. And he's taken to her."

"Yes, she does seem pretty attached to him."

"I am willing to cut my price to $900 for your daughter's sake. How about that?"

My knee-jerk negotiation skills kicked in, "Can you throw in 5 kennel nights for when I travel and don't have anyone to watch him?"

Ralph paused and then, with a hint of admiration in his voice, "That's good. Never had anybody try that before."

"This is what I do, Ralph."

He thought for a minute. "I'll give you two nights, that's it."

I couldn't help myself; always counter a Best and Final. "Can you throw in a bag of dog food?" I pushed it too far.

"I can sell this dog to anyone for full-price and not have to put up with this crap from you. Maybe you'd like it if I went back to my original price?" He barked.

I backpedaled... quickly. "Wait, wait. Sorry, it's just a bad habit. It's almost a natural reflex for me to ask for more. I'll take the deal, $900 and two boarding nights, and be very, very happy."

"Okay... deal."

I gave him my credit card number, and Rocky was ours.

At first, I was angry that Maddy's mom gave away my leverage with that unexpected trip to the pet store. But I came to realize that Ralph might never have given me a discount unless he saw the look on Maddy's face when she was with Rocky.

Ralph cared about his dogs and wanted Rocky to go to the right home. In my tunnel vision approach to getting a good deal, I made the mistake of treating Rocky and his owner the same way customers treat me; as a commodity. I approached the negotiation as a transaction, while Ralph (and Maddy, of course) saw it as a relationship. Without Ralph seeing my daughter and Rocky's connection firsthand, I would have had little leverage. Her mom did me a favor by taking her into the store that day.

So, I kept my promise, got a $300 discount price, and a couple of dog-sitting nights to boot...

...even so, I would have been more satisfied had I gotten that bag of dog food.

Maddy and Rocky the day we brought him home. A smile worth $900, two boarding nights, AND a bag of dog food.

The YKMH Process Summary

Salespeople are good at taking concepts and quickly applying them to their sales process. For that reason, this short summary provides a quick overview of negotiation's three phases, including the strategy and tactics that matter most. I recommend people read the entire book and use the following section as a reference to reinforce the salient points in each of the subsequent chapters.

Negotiations go through three distinct phases. These phases are First Offer, Counteroffers, and Best and Final Offer. In a simple transaction with few items in play, negotiators may go through these steps very quickly: offer-counter-deal. You wouldn't want or need a complex strategy model for negotiating something as simple as a used car. However, in a complicated negotiation with multiple parties and multiple interests, all three steps are crucial.

My negotiation process follows the flow and development of negotiation through these three phases.

First Offers

First Offer Strategy

The best place to start learning how to hold your ground is at the place negotiations typically start; The First Offer. Until the initial offer is on the table, back and forth of negotiation can't proceed. Until that happens, everything else is positioning.

The distance between your First Offer and your Best and Final Offer is the ground you have to give or "wiggle room." The better you hold your ground, the better the deal for you.

Understanding the importance of a strong opening position or First Offer is critical for taking the offensive. Putting a tough customer on the defensive at the beginning makes the rest of the negotiation easier. Prepare to engage with a deliberate and thoughtful approach to protect your profitability and challenge the other side's tactics.

First Offer Tactics

First Offer Tactic #1
Get them to put their number on the table first.

With very few exceptions, you are always better positioned if the customer makes the First Offer. As a rule, being the first to know the gap between you and your opponent puts you in a better position. Knowing how far apart you are before the other side knows gives you an advantage.

Try to avoid making any move before knowing the gap between what they want and what you want. Making counteroffers without knowing this gap is negotiating in the dark. If you can get them to share their starting price or request, even a ballpark number, you are better off. At the very least, you should feel how difficult it will be to close the gap. Why? Because you can revisit your opening bid and revise it up or down relative to your opponent. The number you begin will often define where you end up.

FIRST OFFER TACTIC #2
Make them defend their number.

When and if you can get the other side to reveal their number first, the next step is to pressure them to justify it. Asking the innocent question, "How did you come up with that number?" is a subtle way to go on the offensive and put your opponent on the defensive without seeming confrontational. This question catches tough customers off-guard, puts them psychologically on the defensive, and communicates that you will be a worthy adversary. Challenging the First Offer can be especially effective if their opening position is not well thought out. This tactic is the first step in weakening their position and strengthening yours.

FIRST OFFER TACTIC #3
Conditionally put your number on the table.

After uncovering and challenging their number, you can better determine whether your opening price is too high or too low and adjust your strategy accordingly. If the other side has a weak argument for their opening position, it can allow you to ask for more or offer less.

At some point, however, you have to provide the other side something to work with. Positioning your First Offer as conditional helps you avoid being trapped in a corner. Using a phrase like, "We feel that our offer is fair and reasonable; however, if you want to discuss other possible ways to reach agreement, we are open to that," positions your approach as firm but negotiable. However, once your number is on the table, be prepared for challenges. How will you respond if your opponent asks how you came up with your First Offer or First Counter? How will you respond if the other side asks if your price flexibility? How will you respond to the question, "How firm is your price? The wrong answer is "Firm," but so is the answer, "Negotiable." But what is the right answer?

FIRST OFFER TACTIC #4
Defend your number.

No negotiation guru ever provided me with a good response to the question, "What number do I start with?" They told me, "Every situation is different" or "It's not about who presents the first offer. It's about the level of trust between the two sides."

Give me a break.

It is about the number, and it is about who makes the First Offer, especially if you are in sales.

If you can't answer the question "How did you come up with that price?" or "What makes that fair," it can put you on the defensive. Having a good response to these questions is the first step in defending your number. Hold your ground by having a good explanation of how you arrived at your price. Confidently communicating why your product or service is worth the higher price is crucial to holding your ground. A strong defense communicates to the other side that you will fight to hold your ground. Defending your price is the most critical first step in any negotiation.

Eventually, though, once you know the gap between what you want and what the other side wants, something's got to give. When both sides' numbers are on the table, the only way to close the gap is through offers and counteroffers until you reach some mutually agreeable (or mutually disagreeable) midpoint.

Counteroffers

Counteroffers Strategy

This negotiation phase may be longer or shorter depending on the amount at stake and the number of items in play. In some negotiations, like when purchasing something on Craigslist, just a single counter is the entire negotiation. In a hospital negotiation, both sides can make as many as 30 counteroffers before reaching an agreement.

The Counteroffers phase has the most interplay between strategy and tactics. Being clear on your concession strategy is critical to a good outcome, especially when up against a zero-sum negotiator. The timing of your concessions a critical decision, but even more important is deciding how much to give and how much you ask in return. Improving your skills in this phase will give you better outcomes and more satisfying agreements.

Tough negotiators, when forced to concede, will insist on reciprocity. Experienced and wily purchasing agents never make concessions. They always trade concessions.

Critical to reaching a favorable outcome for your side is establishing the standard of reciprocal value for exchange whenever possible. It is not easy at first, but once you get used to it, it can become second nature. Even if you cannot always get the exact value you relinquished, simply ensuring that you are trading for something will immediately improve most deals.

COUNTEROFFER TACTIC #1
Hard sell every concession.

No concession to a tough customer should ever be made with the comment "Sure. We can do that," even if you can. Concessions should be hard-fought and hard-won. Even a small change in your response, from "Sure, we can do that" to "Sure, we can do that, but not at that price," is a start. Nothing is ever "free" or "no problem" when negotiating with a person who plays hardball. Everything is worth something and therefore should be "traded" for something in kind.

A personal example of this technique is when friends ask me for a copy of my latest book. In the past, I was generous with "absorbing the costs" of these complimentary copies, but I found that many never found the time to read the "gratis" copy; they felt no urgency to read the book. More often, it went to the bottom of their reading list.

Frustrated by their lack of follow-through, I changed my strategy. When asked for a complimentary copy, I offered a deal. I was willing to absorb the book's cost, provided each committed to reading it within a month. Additionally, when I finished reading the book, each had to place a review on my Amazon author Web page. If they fail to follow through, I bill them for the book at a reduced price. Some politely decline my offer, but others read the book and submit an Amazon review.

COUNTEROFFER TACTIC #2
Never concede without getting something in return.

One of the most common mistakes people make in negotiations is to concede more and more ground without making it contingent on reciprocal concessions. It teaches customers to ask for concessions without the expectation of ever having to give up anything in return. Though it seems almost standard in the negotiations I witness, it is very easy to change this mindset.

In some of the larger negotiations in politics and world affairs, it is common for both sides to give up things to reach an agreement. Any bipartisan bill in the US Congress has benefits for both sides. It is almost impossible to get any law passed in any democratic country without concessions to the opposition. The origins of the term horse trading are associated with the Middle East, where shrewd negotiating and hardball tactics are common.

Why not the same in sales?

It isn't necessary to trade price all the time. Flexible contract terms for a standing order or an acceleration of the implementation timeline have monetary values. Becoming good at trading items will significantly improve the profitability of any deal.

COUNTEROFFER TACTIC #3
*Trade the things that cost you the least and
have the most value to the other side.*

Salespeople often make the mistake of conceding more than necessary in a bid to close the sale sooner rather than later. This doesn't need to happen and is corrected with a few quickly learned techniques. Just by knowing which terms and conditions are most important to protect, you can maximize your deal's profitability. Determining the items in play and their value to your opponent helps you create counteroffers that provide you leverage.

Getting the most ground with the least amount of giveaway is the key to dealing with a tough customer. Always trade your least costly for their most valued if you can trade concessions of equal or lesser value to you but the higher value to them that puts you ahead of the game.

If you can get a sale at list price and a "free lunch," take the client to lunch.

COUNTEROFFER TACTIC #4
Challenge their counteroffers.

Tough negotiators rarely expect a challenge to their counters. It can catch them off guard and help you take the offensive even more. The first thing a hard bargainer expects is for you to take the deal on the table once they make their counteroffer. You keep them off balance by challenging them to defend their demands with logic. Asking, "How did you arrive at that counter?" helps you stand your ground, making it harder for the other side to go on the offensive. Forcing the other side to work for every inch is key to reaching an agreement that satisfies your interests. Challenging the offer on the table before you counter is just good negotiating practice.

The back-and-forth, offer-counteroffer-counteroffer makes up the bulk of the negotiation process and can become quite complicated and time-consuming. If you can be both patient and deliberate, you will be more successful.

But at some point, one side runs out of room to maneuver: It is time for a final offer.

BEST AND FINAL OFFERS

Best and Final Offer Strategy

One of the trickiest and most critical parts of the negotiation is holding onto the ground you've been protecting while trying to close the deal. When one side or the other runs out of "wiggle room" or from sheer exhaustion, it may be time to bring the negotiation to a close. Proposing a Best and Final Offer is the technique for concluding negotiation and ending the countering process.

Understanding the core concepts of walk-away option, bottom line, and leverage is crucial for protecting your interests.

BEST AND FINAL OFFER TACTIC #1
Evaluate both sides' walk-away options.

Salespeople sometimes think they are in a weaker negotiation position than they are. They often feel that the buyer has all the power, even if that is not the case. It is understandable, especially if they are behind in their sales numbers and desperate to make a sales quota. However, it is helpful then to remember that there are two sides to this coin.

The important thing to understand is that a true Best and Final Offer means the party who makes that offer is willing to walk away from the deal.

Although you may not have a compelling alternative if the negotiation breaks down, the same may be true of your opponent. In a situation like this, walk-away options become irrelevant because neither party has a good option other than reaching some agreement, regardless of how unpleasant it may be. The key here is that you are only in a weak position if the other side knows you have fewer options than them. And even then, there are tactics to improve your position.

Best and Final Tactic #2
Be the first to ask for their Best and Final Offer.

Of course. You don't ask for a Best and Final Offer at the beginning of a negotiation, but it gives you a tactical advantage when you put the other side on the spot. Asking is much better than being asked.

So, when is the right time to ask for their Best and Final Offer? Although simple negotiations can have one or two counters before a Best and Final Offer, determining when to ask for their final offer in a complex negotiation is more an art than a skill. Figuring this out takes perception and experience, and awareness is key. As offers and counters go back and forth, a good negotiator keeps one eye on the degree to which the gap is closing and the momentum toward an agreement.

BEST AND FINAL OFFER TACTIC #3
Never let them counter your Best and Final Offer.

If you truly make a Best and Final Offer, never, ever make another concession. A true Best and Final Offer means you are willing to let the business go to someone else: You are willing to walk away. To give in and cough up another concession is to weaken your position in this and future negotiations. However, in most industries, I see multiple Best and Final Offers, which negates the term's definition. But it is possible to avoid this pitfall with some very basic tactics and phrases.

BEST AND FINAL OFFER TACTIC #4
Always counter their Best and Final Offer.

It may seem contradictory to the previous "rule" but can be overlooked as a negotiation tactic. When presented with a Best and Final Offer, always ask for "one more thing" to see if their Final Offer is really the other side's best and final. It is a favorite tactic of tough negotiators. Figuring how much you ask for on top of their Final Offer can be tricky. But even if they don't give in, at the very least, you keep them off balance.

About the author

After spending more than 30 years consulting in the areas of sales, negotiation and leadership, Steve retired in Thailand and is following his dream; surfing. Most days you can find him at the beach carving waves, writing and relaxing. Maddy and Rocky still live a happy and relatively carefree life in Seattle.

For information on scheduling a virtual or on-site You're Killing Me Here! Negotiation Workshop, please email him at steve@spjconsulting.com

www.ingramcontent.com/pod-product-compliance
Lightning Source LLC
Chambersburg PA
CBHW060609200326
41521CB00007B/713